INSTANT SCHOOLDAY STARTERS AND FILLERS

by

Ava Deutsch Drutman

SCHOLASTIC
PROFESSIONAL BOOKS

New York • Toronto • London • Auckland • Sydney

For information regarding permission, write to Scholastic Inc., 730 Broadway, New York, NY 10003.

Designed by Intergraphics
Cover design by Vincent Ceci
Cover photography by Richard Hutchings
Illustrations by Joe Chicko, Terri Chicko, Jane McCreary

ISBN 0-590-49116-4

CONTENTS

INTRODUCTION

Welcome to *Instant Schoolday Starters and Fillers*—a book bursting with exciting ways to open the schoolday and fill those few extra moments with fun and stimulation.

Each activity in the book requires minimal preparation and takes just two to ten minutes to complete. Some are designed to reinforce children's higher-level thinking skills; others are designed to make the review of previously learned concepts lively and fun. All will foster an atmosphere of creativity and originality.

The book has been divided into two parts: "Everyday Starters and Fillers" and "Special-Day Starters and Fillers." The activities in the "Everyday" section can be used at any time while those in the "Special-Day" section are designed to be used during specific days of the year.

To meet each teacher's individual classroom management needs, the "Everyday" and "Special Day" sections are both divided into the same four topic areas: (1) At-the-Door Starters contains original ways to greet your students. The activities in this section will start the creative juices flowing the instant students arrive at your classroom door. (2) Desktop Starters and Fillers is, as the name implies, loaded with activities to be performed at desks. (3) Floor Starters and Fillers is chock-full of enjoyable group activities that require the children to sit on—or make use of—the classroom floor. This section also includes several winning ideas for organizing children into groups. (4) Wall Starters and Fillers is brimming with activities that invite children to create or respond to materials that you hang on the wall or the chalkboard.

A number of the activities have been equipped with an **extender** so that you can use them again—either in a follow-up exercise the next day or on several consecutive days. Many contain a **variation**, enabling you to adapt the activity to your specific classroom needs.

Read and enjoy!

EVERYDAY STARTERS AND FILLERS

AT-THE-DOOR STARTERS AND FILLERS

These activities are designed to take place the minute that children arrive at your classroom. They are a way of saying, "Hi!" Some will make children giggle; others will stimulate children's imaginations. Each of them will start your students' day in a very unusual way.

◆ How Many Letters In That Name?

Ask children to tell you the number of letters in their name before they can enter the classroom.

Variation: As children stand in line, ask them how many letters are in the name of the child in front or in back of them.

◆ How's The Weather?

Here's a way to promote awareness of the changing weather. Before children can enter the room, have them tell you a word that describes that day's weather.

Variation: Invite children to tell you a word that describes the previous day's weather.

◆ Who Has The Same Color Hair?

Do you know the color of a friend's hair or eyes? After this starter, the children in your class will. Before children arrive at school, write all the possible colors of hair on the chalkboard. Tell children not to sit at their desks, but instead to find the color of their hair on the chalkboard. Have children with the same color hair gather in groups under their color. Appoint one child to count the number of children in each group and then write it below their color on the board. What color is the most common? Discuss the results with your students. Don't forget to join the group that has your hair color!

Variation: This activity is fun to do with eye color too.

◆ What Time Is It?

Here's an enjoyable way to practice telling time. As each child arrives, ask him to tell you the time that appears on your watch (or a clock) before entering the room. If you have digital and analog watches available, alternate between the two.

◆ Counting Shoelace Holes

Surprise! Ask students to tell you how many holes for laces there are in their shoes. The lucky child who didn't wear sneakers won't have to count at all.

♦ Hot And Cold

Here's a delightful way to review the concepts of hot and cold. Duplicate the ticket (page 107). As children enter the room, present them each with a ticket. Ask half the children to write something that is very cold on the ticket; ask the other half to write something that is very hot. Explain to children that later in the day they will have to hand in their tickets to participate in another curriculum-based activity.

♦ Name That Animal Sound

This is a good way to enhance listening skills. Before each child enters, whisper the name of an animal in her ear. Then ask her to make that animal sound. The child standing behind that child must name the animal. After the animal is named, the child may go into the room.

♦ Suggestion Box

Set up a suggestion box. As children come into the room ask them if they have suggestions for the class such as books to read, projects to do, etc. If so, give them a slip of paper on which to write the suggestion. This can be dropped in the suggestion box and discussed later.

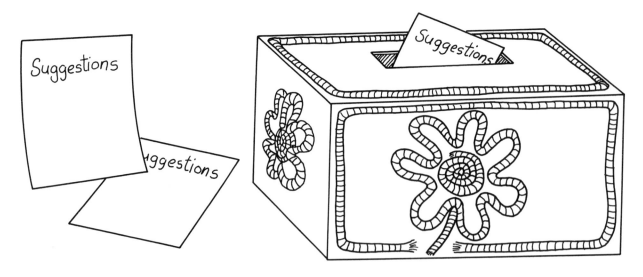

◆ Wild Walk-Ins

Try this vocabulary development starter that's simply fun.
Each day demonstrate an interesting or unusual way of
walking such as gliding, striding, tiptoeing, strutting, etc.
After demonstrating and saying the word that describes
the action, ask children to enter the class demonstrating
that word.

◆ Put Your Hand Here

Here's a following-directions starter to try that reinforces
positional words. Whisper a direction for each child to follow
as he/she enters the classroom such as the following:

- Put your hand *on* your head.
- Put your hand right *under* your chin.
- Put your hand *behind* your ear.
- Put your hand *over* your head.

Ask children to keep their hands in place until they reach
their seats.

◆ Entry Ticket

Intrigue children by telling them that tomorrow they will need a special ticket to enter the classroom. Explain that this ticket will be the name of a favorite book and why it is their favorite. The next day, as children appear at the classroom door, collect their entry ticket by listening.

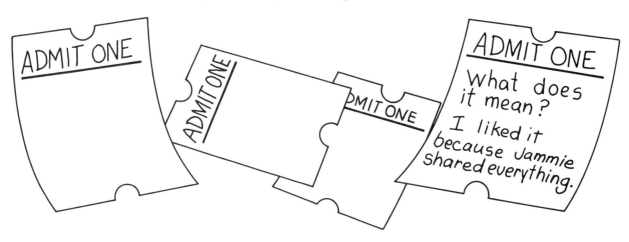

◆ Every Color Of The Rainbow

Rainbows always delight children. Tell children that tomorrow they will be bringing a rainbow into the classroom! Assign each child a color of the rainbow. Then tell them to bring something of that color to school. The next day, have all the students show their colored item to you before entering the room. If your school hallways permit, have all the children with red items assemble in a group, all the children with blue items assemble in another group, and so on. Then invite each group into the room in the order of the colors of the rainbow.

◆ Magical Twigs

Put a little magic into your morning. Invite children to bring Magical Twigs to school tomorrow. Explain that they should find the twigs outside. As children appear at the door, have them show you their Magical Twigs. If some children can't find any they can share with others who did. Before they can enter ask them each to tell you one magical thing the twig can do.

◆ Turning Words Into Actions

How often do you wish you could turn your words into actions? Give your students the opportunity to do this by providing them with action words. As each child arrives, whisper a verb that tells him how to enter the room. For example: hop, skip, jump, walk, stroll, or jog.

◆ Name That Synonym

Start the day with a little vocabulary building. As each child appears at the door, whisper a word that has an obvious synonym. Have him whisper the synonym to you.

Variation: This activity can be done with antonyms and homonyms too.

◆ An Aerobic A.M.

Start your students' day aerobically. As children arrive, stop them at the classroom door and ask them to jog slowly to their seats. Once at their seats, you might encourage them to jog in place for one minute.

◆ A Smile A Day

Before children can enter your classroom, they need to give you a smile.

Variation: Ask children to do one of the following things in order to enter the room.

- Say hello
- Say hello in a foreign language
- Slap you five
- Shake your hand
- Greet you in an unusual way
- Frown, grimace, look surprised, etc.

◆ Name A Pet

As each child enters, have her whisper the name of an unusual animal she would like to have as a pet.

Extender: Have the children write down the animal they selected. Then read each animal name and have the class guess who wrote it.

◆ I'm Happy To Be In School Because . . .

Here's a way to learn what every child enjoys in school. As each child enters the room, have him complete this sentence:

"I'm happy to be in school because _____."

◆ Animal Acts

Ever dreamed of being an animal? Your students probably have. As children arrive, ask them to choose an animal. Then encourage them to move toward their desk as that animal would. Invite the next student on line to identify the animal.

◆ Parts Of Speech Tickets

Here's a quick way to review the parts of speech. Duplicate the reproducible ticket (page 107.) Give each child a ticket. Ask her to write an example of the part of speech you are presently studying on it. The next day, have students give you the tickets as they enter the room.

Variation: This exercise can be done with phonics skills as well.

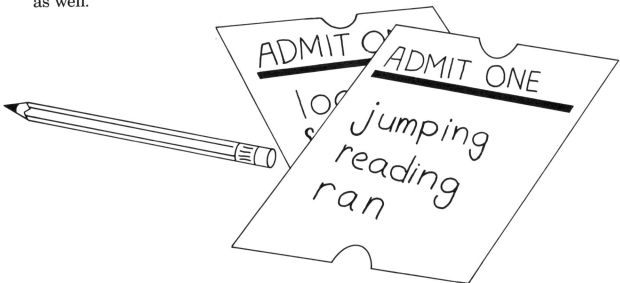

◆ Follow My Directions

Here's a way to have children enter the room that always brings a lot of smiles. As children enter the room, give them directions such as "Continue taking two giant steps and three baby steps until you reach your desk."

Variation: Have the next child on line give the directions.

◆ Summer Dreams

As the school year comes to an end, all children dream of what they will do with their free time. Encourage children to share their dreams of summer by each whispering one wish to you.

◆ How Does This Feel?

Here's a way to make children more aware of their valuable sense of touch. Round up a few objects (or textured fabrics) for the children to touch. Since the sense of touch is heightened when people cannot see, put the objects in a bag or tell children to close their eyes. As each child enters the room, have him touch an object. Ask him to use one word to describe what he feels. Can he guess what the object is?

◆ What Do You Think This Story Will Be About?

This simple starter will make children look forward to the reading segment of the day. As each child enters, quietly state the title of the story she will be reading during reading time. Ask her to think about what might happen in the story.

◆ Identify That Sound

Ask children to walk into the classroom, sit down, and listen with their eyes closed. Then make a sound by snapping your fingers, clapping your hands, or stamping your feet. Have children identify the sound and tell how you made it.

Variation: Tap different items in the room. Then have children identify the objects that were tapped.

◆ Music And Your Imagination

This activity will bring a little classical music into your room. As children enter, have a classical record or tape playing. If you pick a piece that evokes a special feeling or image for you, your students will probably have similar responses to it. Encourage children to sit at their desks and close their eyes while listening. Then invite them to share what they saw in their minds as the music played.

Variation: Play the music and have the children describe how the music made them feel.

◆ Clap Your Hands To That Beat

Looking for an activity guaranteed to snap children out of any early morning doldrums? Try this one. As children enter the room, play a record or tape that has a steady rhythm. Stand at the door and clap your hands to the beat. As children enter, invite them to clap their hands to the rhythm along with you. Encourage them to continue clapping even when they have reached their seats.

◆ Use The Clue And Draw Your Idea

Here's a way to begin the day with children thinking creatively. Give the children one general clue and see how many different responses you can get. For instance, you might say, "It lives in the sea," to each child as they enter the room. Hand them each a sheet of drawing paper and make crayons available. Ask children to draw their responses to the clue. You'll be amazed at the variety of sea creatures and plants they create.

Extender: On a bulletin board, display children's artwork under the clue.

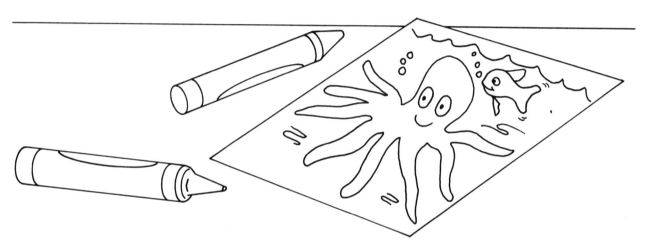

◆ Name That Teacher

How well do the children in your class know the teachers in the school? As they arrive, state a grade. Ask children to name a teacher who teaches that grade.

◆ Litter Collections

Try this filler. The result will be a cleaner room. Pause for a moment and ask students to look for litter. They can look on the floor or in their desk. Encourage children to figure out whether the litter can be recycled. If there is no way to recycle it, have them put the litter in an empty trash can. You'll be surprised to see how full the trash can gets.

◆ My Favorite Tune

Everyone has a special song. As children arrive, ask them to tell you their favorite song. Then you tell them yours.

◆ Name That Prefix

Think fast! State a word that has a prefix in it. Count to five. Ask the first arriving student to name the prefix. If he can't name it, he has to go to the end of the line. Then ask the second arriving student to name the prefix of a different word, and so on. Be sure to match the difficulty of the task to each individual's skill level. You probably won't want to send a student to the end of the line more than once. This exercise will really keep students on their toes!

Variation: Perform this activity using suffixes or root words.

◆ What's In Your Book Bag?

Children will be amazed to find out how many things they have in their book bags. As children arrive, ask them to tell you how many things they think are in their book bags. After children have reached their seats, ask them to check to see if they were right.

◆ Count Your Steps

"Go directly from this door to your desk. Do not stop to talk! Do not stop at the pencil sharpener!" Invite children to count the number of steps they take from the classroom door to their desks.

Variation: 1. Ask children to find the shortest route from the classroom door to their desks. This might take several attempts so allow children to try only one path each morning.
             2. Ask children to find the longest path to their desks.

◆ Silly Hat Happening

Invite children to wear silly hats to school on a specific day. Tell them to put on their silly hats before they enter the classroom. Once children are seated, encourage them to quickly state what they think makes their hats silly.

◆ Turning Yarn Into Worms

All you need for this activity is a three- to five-inch piece of yarn for each student in your class. As children enter, give each of them a piece of yarn. Tell them that these are their pet worms. Ask each child to find a special place for the worm at her desk.

Variation: Invite children to name their worms.

Extender: Have each child create a drawing of a home and environment for her worm. Then have her paste the worm into the home.

◆ Where Do You Live?

Do most children know where they live? Find out with this activity. As children enter, ask them a variety of questions about where they live. The questions can be very specific such as, "What is the name of your street?" or very general such as, "What is the name of the planet you live on?"

◆ What Color Is Your Clothing?

Children are always fascinated by this starter. As children arrive, have them close their eyes. Then ask them to name the color of a specific item of clothing they are wearing. You and the children will be quite entertained by the responses. (Of course, it is always well to remember which children have trouble remembering such things and not put them on the spot.)

◆ Name That Color Object

Do you think of an apple when someone says red? See what things your students think of when you mention a color. As each student arrives, say a color. Then ask him to name something that is that color before he enters the room.

◆ Cloud Formations

Two people seldom see the same image in a cloud. On a day when the sky is full of clouds, ask children to look at them and to tell you what they see. You'll be surprised by the wide variety of responses.

◆ Backwards Spelling

Here's a silly start to the day. Have children spell their own name backwards before they go into the classroom. For children who have trouble, write their name on a slip of paper and let them read the name backwards. This will ensure success for all.

◆ Three Words, Same Letter

Here is an enjoyable way to review the alphabet as well as initial letter sounds. As children arrive at school, assign them each a different letter of the alphabet. Encourage each child to think of three words that begin with that letter. After everyone has arrived, invite students to tell the class their three words. If you have less than 26 students, assign some of them two letters. If you have more than 26 students, have some of them work with partners.

◆ Foreign Hellos

Each day say hello to your students in a different language. Then encourage them to repeat the foreign greeting. Tell children what language the word comes from. Encourage them to say hello to one another in that language.

African (Swahili): jambo
French: bonjour
Hebrew: shalom

Japanese: konnichiwa
Native American (Cherokee): o si yo
Spanish: hola

◆ Remembering The Morning

Trying to remember what you did before you came to school is not always easy. Get children's thinking skills working by asking them to remember the very first thing they did after they woke up that morning.

Variation: Have children share a funny thing that happened on the way to school, an exciting thing, or what the first words they said when they woke up were.

◆ Animals And Their Homes Game

Here's a quick way to review animal habitats. State the name of an animal and ask a child to name the place where it lives. For example:

You ask, "Where does a bear live?"

A child can respond, "A bear lives in a cave."

or

"A bear lives in a zoo."

or

"A bear lives in a forest."

If the child responds correctly, he gets to enter the room. If he does not know, ask the next child the same question, while the first child listens.

Variation: A simpler version of this game is for you to state a habitat and have children name an animal that lives there. Animal habitats include: a house, a farm, a jungle, a swamp, and a rain forest.

◆ As Big As Your Thumb?

"What if you were only as big as your thumb? How would you get up to your seat?" Puzzle children with this question as they enter the room. Once everyone is inside, encourage children to share their solutions to this unusual problem.

Variation: Build on this idea by asking: (1) "How would you eat lunch?" (2) "How would you hold a pencil?" (3) "How would you be able to make your voice loud enough to be heard in class?" Encourage imaginative responses.

◆ Know Your States

Here's a way to encourage children to get to know a state or two. Tell children that you want them to find out the name of at least one state—other than their own—by tomorrow. As they enter the room the next day, ask them to name a state or two.

◆ Favorite Foods

Start the day with unusual and thought-provoking idea. If you could speak to your teeth, how do you think they would answer this question:

"Which food do you enjoy chewing the most?"

Everyone will be entertained by the question and the responses.

◆ Imagine You're A Bug

Many children enjoy watching and handling bugs. How many of them think about what it would be like to be a bug? Ask half the children to imagine that they are flying bugs. Ask the other half to pretend they are crawling bugs. Where would they stay in your classroom?

Extender: After everyone is seated, you might wish to discuss why they chose the locations they did. Would a flying bug choose a different spot than a crawling one?

◆ Beans In The Hand

Everybody loves to guess how many beans are in a jar. Here's a new twist on that traditional guessing game. As students enter the room, give them a handful of beans. Ask them to immediately guess how many beans are in their hands. Then tell them to take the beans to their seats and count how many beans were actually in their hands.

Note: Other tiny objects, such as buttons or beads, can be used instead of beans.

Extender: Add the beans up, put them all in a jar, and give it to another class to estimate the number.

◆ Preventing Tooth Decay

No one wants to get cavities. Promote good dental care with this lighthearted activity. Duplicate the big tooth (page 111). As children arrive, give them a copy of the big tooth. Ask them to name the tooth and then write something on the tooth that it likes and something that it doesn't like. Ask children to cut out teeth and tape them on a mouth drawn on a chalkboard or bulletin board. The class can then read all the ideas. (This activity could be done during Dental Health Month in February.)

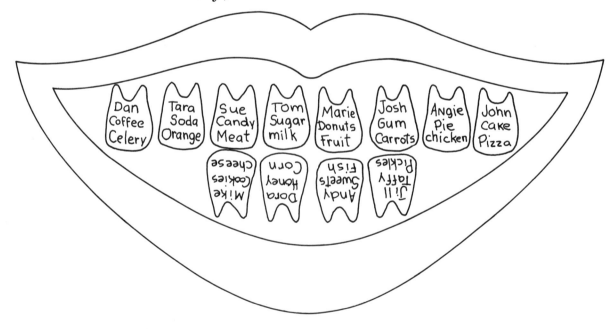

DESKTOP STARTERS AND FILLERS

This group of activities will delight and motivate children. Every one is designed for students to do at their own desks. As children come into the room, have materials needed available on their desks. Children can work individually or in pairs. Here's to pleasant moments during the day!

◆ Observing Leaves

Here's a way to bring a little of the great outdoors into your classroom. Place a leaf on each child's desk. Then, before children enter the room, write the following questions on the chalkboard.

- What color is it?
- What is it the same size as?
- How does it smell?
- How does it feel?

Encourage children to think about these questions as they study their leaves. Then encourage each child to compare her leaf to one belonging to a classmate.

Variation: A pebble can be placed on each desk instead of a leaf. Invite children to study the features of their pebbles.

◆ Feel The Rhythm

Here is another entertaining way to enhance listening skills. Write a familiar poem or nursery rhyme on the chalkboard. Organize your students into two groups. Have one group read the poem aloud in unison. Invite the other groups to mark the rhythm by clapping hands, stamping feet, and snapping fingers.

◆ Make A Crayon Alphabet

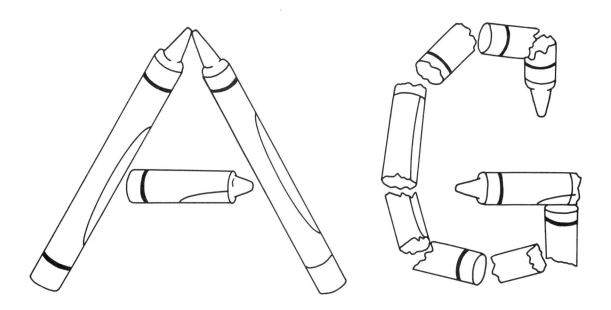

Here's an unusual way for your students to use crayons to learn the alphabet. Make sure every child has at least ten crayons. Ask them each to assemble a letter of the alphabet using the crayons. Tell children that they can create most of the letters without breaking any crayons. (Letters with curved parts, such as G and Q, however, can be made by using little bits of broken crayons.) If children are struggling, demonstrate how to form a few letters. Once each child has made a letter, ask him to create another one. Before you know it, you'll have colorful letters on top of every desk.

◆ Identifying Hidden Sounds

Sometimes there are so many sounds going on at once that children can't distinguish one noise from all the others. This activity will help them to isolate a single sound. Hide an object that makes a continuous noise. It could be a radio that is turned on softly, a clock that ticks, or an audio tape that is playing. As children enter the room, describe the sound to them. Ask them to locate the sound and stand near it. Can anyone guess what object is making the sound? If time permits, have children take turns hiding the object. Then ask other classmates to find it.

◆ Find The Letters Of The Alphabet

This exercise is especially useful for classes that have just learned the alphabet. Cut every letter of the alphabet out of cardboard or construction paper. Hide the letters around the room. As each child arrives, tell her a letter of the alphabet. Ask her to find that letter in the room. When everyone has completed the search, invite children to stand with their letters in alphabetical order.

Variaton: This activity can also be done with words and numbers.

◆ Creating Number Creatures

Zap! This unique activity turns numbers into silly creatures. Each student will need a sheet of drawing paper and a pencil. Write the numbers zero through nine on the chalkboard. Ask each child to choose her favorite number. Then tell students to imagine that their numbers are turning into creatures. Have them close their eyes and ask them these questions:

• Does your creature have legs?
• Does it have a face?
• Is it a special color?
• Is it friendly?

Then ask children to draw their creatures. If children are having difficulty, demonstrate by turning a four into a creature (as shown above).

◆ Your Own Magic Seed

Get those creative juices flowing with this simple activity. Place a sheet of drawing paper and a seed on each child's desk. (Any kind of seed will do.) Ask children to imagine that they are going to plant the seeds. What would each seed grow up to be? Have children draw pictures to illustrate what their seeds will become. Then invite children to form small groups and share their ideas.

Extender: Plant the seeds with the children. Let them find out what their seeds grow into and compare those plants to what the children imagined. Encourage every child to discuss which result he liked better—the imaginary one or the real one.

◆ Start Your Creation With A Big Black Dot

Sometimes all it takes is a little black dot to stimulate children's creativity. Begin by placing a black paper circle approximately $1\frac{1}{2}$ inches (or 4 centimeters) in diameter on each child's desk along with a blank piece of drawing paper, glue, and markers or crayons. Tell children to place the circle anywhere they like on the paper and to affix it with glue. Then invite each child to use the circle as part of a drawing. Have them draw something specific such as an animal, a vehicle, or a toy, or let children's imaginations run free.

Extender: Invite children to share their completed drawings with the class.

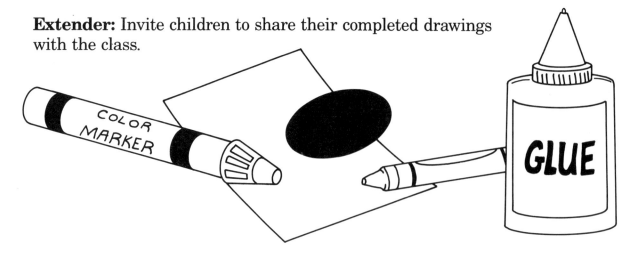

◆ Which Is Larger?

Help children discover how the same thing often comes in a variety of sizes. Organize children into pairs. Ask children to take out three of the same objects from their desks such as three pencils, three crayons, three notebooks, or three books. Invite children to determine which object is the largest and which object is the smallest. Have children place their own objects next to each other in order of size. Then ask the students to look at their partner's objects and see if they agree with the order.

◆ Imagine You Are A Color

Everyone has a favorite color. What if a child could be that color? Each student will need a sheet of drawing paper, markers or crayons, and imagination! Write the following sentences on the chalkboard for your students to read:

• Imagine that you are a color.
• You could be any color.
• Would you be a pale sky blue?
• Would you be a bright green tree?
• Would you be a small dot of color?
• Would you fill the entire page?
• Draw yourself as a color.

◆ Neat-And-Clean Desks

Sooner or later, most children's desks get messy. Here's a simple checklist that will solve the problem. Duplicate the Neat-and-Clean Desk Checklist (page 30). Give each child a copy. Have them follow each step, checking it off when it is completed. (If children's desks are really messy then this project could take up to a half an hour.)

Neat-And-Clean Desk Checklist

It's easy to find things when your desk is neat. Follow these steps for a neat desk. Check each step off after you do it.

1. ☐ Take everything out of your desk.

2. ☐ Think about what can be recycled or given to another classmate.

3. ☐ Throw away anything that you do not need or that is broken. Put these things in the garbage can.

4. ☐ Make sure your books have covers. If a book doesn't have a cover, you might want to take it home and cover it. Ask your teacher first.

5. ☐ Sharpen any pencils with broken points.

6. ☐ Put all your crayons in their box.

7. ☐ Put any loose papers in your notebook or folder.

Have you completed steps 1–7? If your answers is yes, then you are ready to follow steps 8–12.

8. ☐ Put the covered books neatly back in the desk.

9. ☐ Put your notebooks and folders neatly back in the desk.

10. ☐ Place your box of crayons in the desk.

11. ☐ Place your pencils and pens where you can reach them. You may want to put them in a pencil case.

12. ☐ If you have anything else, put it neatly in your desk. Congratulations! You did a great job!

◆ Can You Measure With Your Hands?

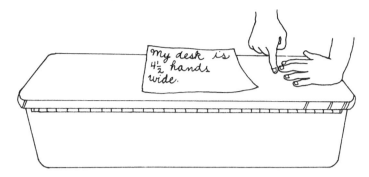

This activity will help your class understand how ancient civilizations measured things before rulers were invented. Invite children to use their hands to measure their desks. Before children enter the room, write the following questions on the chalkboard.

• How many hands long is your desk?
• How many hands wide is your desk?

Have children use the length of their hands to measure the width and length of their desk. Have children compare results. If results differ, have children compare hand sizes. Help them conclude that the results differ because their hands are different sizes.

Variation: 1. Have children use the width of their hands, or the spread between their thumbs and forefingers to measure their desks. Then have them compare the results.
2. Give children other objects to measure the width and length of their desk. Possible objects include: pencils, crayons, or paper clips.

◆ Five Dollars For Food

Getting the most food for your money is no easy task. With careful planning, children can learn this skill. As children enter the room, have them choose a partner. Give each pair a weekly supermarket flyer. Tell children that they have five dollars to spend on food. Duplicate the play money (page 110) and give each child the equivalent of five dollars. Then have them choose what they want to buy. Remind them that they cannot spend more than five dollars.

♦ Alphabetical Objects

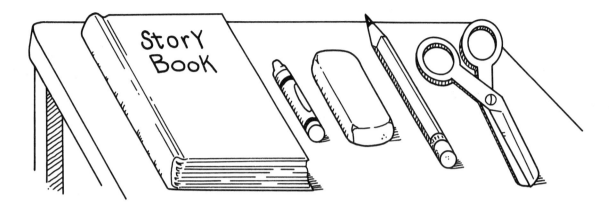

Surprise your children by placing at least five different items on each set of desks. Those items might be: a book, a pencil, a crayon, an eraser, and a pair of safety scissors. Ask the children who sit at each set of desks to work together to put the objects in alphabetical order. If children are having difficulty, remind them of the method used to alphabetize words. Circulate around the room, checking for the correct order.

Extender: 1. Have children add their own items to the ones you selected and then alphabetize them.

2. Have children choose items for each other to alphabetize.

♦ Name The Names

How many names can your students think of that begin with the letter *A*? As children arrive, give them each a different letter and a sheet of paper. Ask them to write down all the names they can think of that begin with those letters. Circulate around the room to make sure that all the names on their lists begin with the right letters. Remember to use only letters that frequently appear at the beginning of names.

Variation: Ask children to make a list of only boy's names, only girl's names, or last names.

◆ Nouns In A Bowl

Say the word *monster* and many children will think of words like "scary" and "ugly" to name just two. Give children the opportunity to reach inside their minds and gather the many words they associate with a single noun. You can do this by writing nouns on index cards. Write one noun on each card. Place the cards in a bowl. Make sure there are enough index cards so that every child can have at least one. As children enter the room, ask them each to reach in and take one card. Then ask them to close their eyes and picture their nouns. Encourage children to make lists of all the words that enter their minds.

Thirty Suggested Nouns:

princess	baseball	school	tree	bird
cat	friend	tiger	monster	truck
fireman	doctor	mountains	bus	king
banana	policeman	carrot	rainbow	elephant
apple	sink	ladder	sandwich	house
pencil	television	circus	car	camera

Extender: Have children write stories using their lists of words.

Variation: Instead of giving nouns, provide children with verbs or adjectives.

Thirty Suggested Verbs:

smile	shout	forget	ride	paint
run	talk	leap	talk	cry
sew	wander	shrink	help	climb
dance	laugh	sweep	remember	grab
throw	cook	bite	draw	sing
swim	sit	crawl	fight	hide

Thirty Suggested Adjectives:

beautiful	cold	clever	friendly	ugly
wild	funny	joyful	tiny	huge
curious	hungry	colorful	cloudy	sad
soft	round	hot	brave	warm
strong	tremendous	empty	serious	fearful
dark	shiny	gentle	young	old

◆ Math Matters

Children always enjoy this starter because it makes learning number facts fun. As children enter the room, give each of them an index card with a number or a math sign on it. Then invite children to circulate around the room and group themselves so that they form correct math sentences. For example, if your class is presently studying the addition facts for *4*, you could hand out the following index cards:

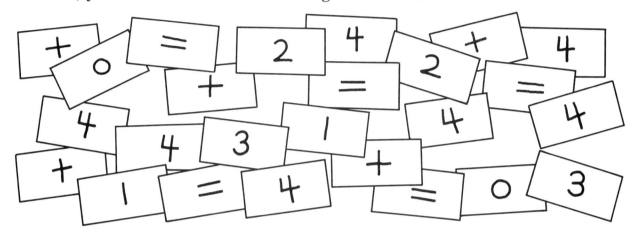

Variations: Ask children to form groups. Give each group some blank index cards. Challenge children to work together to create their own math facts.

◆ If I Were . . .

Here's a filler that will really get your class in a creative mood. Each child will need a blank sheet of paper, and a pencil, crayon or marker. Engage children in creative thought by asking them to imagine they are each a vegetable. Give them a few moments to decide which vegetable they would like to be. Then invite children to draw pictures of themselves as those vegetables.

Variation: Have children imagine they are four-legged animals, pieces of furniture, or fruits.

◆ Thank You

How about having each student thank someone just for the fun of it? Duplicate the piece of lined stationery (page 36). Place a sheet of stationery on each child's desk. Ask children to think of someone in the class who they care about or has been kind to them. Ask each child to write a thank-you note to that special person. Finally, encourage children to give their notes to those people.

Extender: Have children color in the design on the stationery's border.

◆ Me, Myself And I

Sometimes children don't appreciate themselves enough. Here's an activity that helps children to realize how very special they are. Duplicate the piece of lined stationery (page 36). Place a piece of stationery on each child's desk. Then ask children to think about what they like about themselves. Have children make lists of all their positive traits on the paper.

Extender: Save each child's list. When they are feeling blue, they can reread the lists.

◆ Get Well Soon

This starter will help bond classmates to each other. Sometimes children are absent from school for more than a few days with an illness. Duplicate the lined stationery (pages 36). Distribute a piece to all students and tell them to write short get-well notes to their absent classmate. The brief notes will bring a little cheer to the classmate who is ill. They will also foster a caring spirit in the classroom.

◆ Complete The Comic

This idea combines creative writing and deductive logic. Cut out a comic strip and cover the words in the last box. As children enter, have them choose partners. Give each pair a copy of the comic strip. Tell them they have two minutes to brainstorm what the characters in the last box might be saying. Then ask students to write those words in the box.

Extender: Invite students to share their completed strips with the class. You'll be surprised at what they come up with.

◆ Mail The Letter

Use this starter to reinforce reading skills. Put a "mailbox" in front of your room. On the mailbox, display one phonics skill that the children are presently studying. For example, if you have just finished studying the suffix *tion*, then *tion* should appear on the mailbox. As children enter, give each one a "postcard" to mail. Tell them that in order to mail their cards, they must write at least one word that ends with the suffix *tion*. Then have them put their postcards in the mailbox.

Extender: Read aloud or display the postcards.

◆ Comparing Coins

People use coins everyday, but rarely notice the interesting designs on them. Place a sheet of blank paper and a coin on each child's desk. Do not put the same coin on adjacent desks. Have children look at both sides of the coin. Then ask children to compare their coins with their neighbors' coins. Encourage children to discuss ways in which their coins are the same and ways in which they are different.

◆ Communicating With Pebble Pals

This activity will help shy students speak to others. Put a pebble on each child's desk. Ask children to name their pebbles. Then invite students to introduce their pebbles to their neighbors. Encourage children to pretend their pebbles are communicating with each other.

◆ What's This?

Bring in odd objects that don't have immediately recognizable uses. Divide students into small groups. Ask each group to think of all the possible uses each thing could have. After this brainstorming, discuss ideas. Then you can reveal the real identity and uses of the objects.

FLOOR STARTERS AND FILLERS

Here is a group of activities intended to give children a break from their desks. You will find that there are two types of Floor Starters and Fillers. First, there are activities designed to take place on—or make use of—the classroom floor. Then there are activities designed to be done in groups. They have been placed in this section because one desk cannot accommodate a group of children.

◆ Alphabetical Order

Here's an activity that reinforces alphabetizing and organizational skills. Duplicate the footstep (page 109). Print one letter of the alphabet on each footstep. As children enter the room give a footstep to each of them. Ask children to find the classmate who has the letter that comes before and after theirs. Then have children work together to place the footsteps in alphabetical order in the front of the classroom.

◆ The Tile Count

Here's an activity that young children always enjoy. Draw their attention to the tiles on the floor as they enter the room. Surprise children by asking them to count the number of tiles on the floor. When they are finished compare their results.

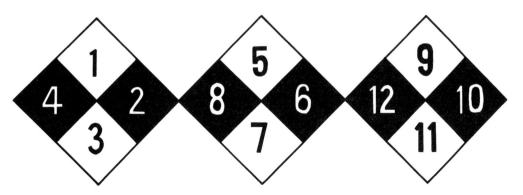

◆ Follow The Footsteps

Children love to follow footsteps! Delight children by
beginning their day with this starter. Duplicate the footsteps
(page 109). Attach footsteps to the floor leading to a spot in
the room where you want the children to gather. As children
enter the room, simply ask them to follow the footsteps!

◆ Solve The Problem And Find The Answer

This exercise will prepare children for multiple-choice
questions. Write several math problems on the chalkboard.
Write the answers on cards or the footsteps (page 109). Hide
the correct answers along with several incorrect "decoy"
answers. Invite each child to solve a problem. Then
encourage him to search the room to find the card or footstep
with the correct answer printed on it. After each child has
found an answer, have him return to his seat to display it.

◆ Toss It

Some days children need a physical activity to get them
started. Here's one that also reinforces counting skills. Pair
off children as they enter the room. Give each pair a ball
of yarn, a foam ball, or any type of ball that can be used
indoors. Ask children to toss the ball back and forth. Tell
them to count the number of times they can toss it without
letting it drop.

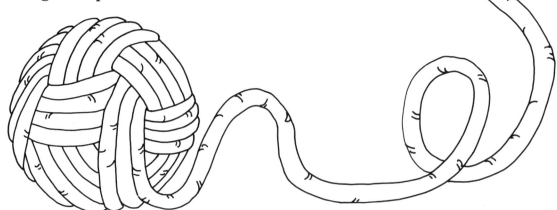

◆ Toss And Add

When nasty weather makes recess an impossibility, this filler will provide a much-needed outlet for physical activity. Duplicate the footsteps (page 109). Write numbers on the footsteps and attach them to the floor. Have children toss a ball of yarn, a foam ball, or any type of ball that can be used indoors at the numbers. Tell children to hit two numbers. Then have them add the numbers up. If you have more than fifteen children in your class, it is best to have them work in pairs.

◆ Are You Listening Carefully?

This exercise helps children to listen carefully and speak clearly. Have children sit on the floor in pairs. Ask each child to tell his partner one thing that he did the evening before. Ask the listener to restate what his partner just told him. If he remembers the information correctly, have the first child tell him something else that he did during the evening. Once again have the listener speak. This time he must state both things that the child did during evening. Then ask the students to switch roles.

◆ Counting Claps

Here's a starter that reinforces counting and listening skills. Organize children into pairs. Have one child in the pair think of a secret number between one and twenty. Tell the child to clap her hands that number of times. Have the other child state the total number of claps. Then ask the partners to switch roles.

◆ Colorful Patterns Of Feet

The ability to distinguish patterns helps children to better understand the order of the world around them. Here is a simple way to acquaint children with this concept. Duplicate the footsteps (page 109) and assign every child a specific color. Have children take home their footsteps to color. The following day, collect all the footsteps. Place them on the floor in patterns. Then challenge children to identify the patterns. For example, the pattern might be: yellow, blue, red; yellow, blue, red.

Variation: 1. Have children create their own patterns.
2. Place numbers or letters in the footsteps. Arrange them in patterns.

◆ Match It

Matching is a skill most children can perform easily. Start the day with this success-oriented activity. Create your own cards or use a store-bought set of cards for this activity. You will need a pair of matching cards for every student in the class. Make sure no student's cards have the same image as those of a classmate. As children enter the room, give each of them a card. Have a matching card hanging on the wall. Tell children to find their match. If you choose to create your own cards, you can use them to help teach phonics and a sight-word vocabulary.

◆ **Let's Organize Into Groups**

Children love to work in groups. The activities that follow will require children to form groups. The recommended group size is four to six children. Here are some ways to let your students know which group is theirs. (More elaborate methods can be used more than once.)

1. Duplicate the hands (page 108) or feet (page 109). Write each child's name on one. Organize the names in groups. As the first child in each group enters the room, give that person the rest of the names in the group. Make that child responsible for gathering the others.

2. Decide which child will be in each group. Prepare markers of different colors for each group. Then place a sign of the same color in a spot where you want the group to meet. As each child enters the room, give him a color and ask him to find the location where that color group is meeting.

3. Duplicate the hands (page 108) or feet (page 109). Write each child's name on one. Display them in a cluster under the group's number.

4. Arrange the groups based on children's birthday months or birthday seasons.

5. Use heavy-gauge poster board and felt to create a Group Board. Glue felt pockets to the board. Write the name of each child on a pocket. On cards that fit in the pockets, write group numbers. Place one card in each child's pocket. Display the board on the days you wish to have children form groups. Then as children enter room, have them check their pockets to find out which groups they are in.

TODAY'S GROUP BOARD

Ron   Alice   John   José   Kim

◆ Left Directions, Right Directions

Group Activity

Here's an enjoyable way to help children learn the difference between their left and right. It will also foster a sense of team spirit. Organize the children into groups. Ask for a volunteer to lead each group. Have leaders come up so you can give them each a direction. Then have them return to their groups and each call out the direction. All the other children must follow it. Here are some possible directions to give group leaders:

Face the left.	Hop on your left foot.
Face the right.	Hop on your right foot.
Raise your left hand.	Touch your left ear.
Raise your right hand.	Touch your right ear.

Encourage the members of each group to help one another follow the directions.

◆ A Noisy Silence

Group Activity

It's unusual to hear the sounds of silence. But this unique activity gives your children the rare opportunity. Organize children into groups. Have each group sit very quietly. Ask them to listen for sounds in the classroom, in the hall, and outside. Invite children to list all the sounds they hear.

Extender: Tell one student to start to talk softly. Then ask another and another to speak. Ask children to observe the point at which they can no longer hear the sounds of silence.

Sounds of Silence
1. Birds Singing
2. Water running in the pipes
3. Air Conditioning
4. Wind blowing

◆ Yesterday And Last Night

Group Activity

Divide students into groups to chat. Ask them to discuss
what they did after school yesterday and last night. After a
few minutes of discussion, survey activities and tally the
variety in a simple chalkboard tally.

◆ A Ten-Headed Monster

Group Activity

Here's an easy way for students to create an amusing collage.
For this filler, you'll need an abundant supply of magazines,
paste, and safety scissors. You'll also need a large sheet of
paper with a headless monster drawn on it. Organize
children into groups. Have the groups cut heads and faces
out of the magazines. Then encourage each group to paste
the ten heads on the monster's body. You might also give
children the option to draw some of the heads. Promote
cooperation while the groups arrange the heads on the
monsters' bodies. Voilà, each group has its very own monster.

Variation: Choose the number
of heads based on the number
of children in each group.

◆ Finish The Picture Puzzle

Group Activity

Since most children love putting puzzles together, here's a "puzzling" activity for them. This activity takes a little bit of preparation. Remove several pictures from magazines and cut each one into fourths. Create piles made up of pieces from two or three pictures, give each pile a number, and put them all on the floor. Organize children into number groups. Invite children to find their numbers on the floor. Explain to them that there are pieces of two (or three) different pictures in each pile. Challenge the children to work with their groups to put the pictures back together. If necessary, give children a hint that there are four parts needed to complete each picture.

◆ The Perfect Sandwich

Group Activity

Give your students the opportunity to make perfect sandwiches—with crayons and paper that is! Provide paper and pencils, markers, or crayons. Divide students into groups. Then let the fun begin. Invite each group to work together to draw and describe the perfect sandwich.

Variation: Here are some other types of sandwiches you can ask the groups to create.

1. The Most Beautiful Sandwich
2. The Most Disgusting Sandwich
3. The Largest Sandwich
4. The Favorite-Things Sandwich

◆ It's In The Telephone Book

Using the telephone book requires a variety of skills. Here's an unbeatable way to help children develop them. Organize children into groups. Give every group a local telephone book. Have children locate their names in the book. Ask them to make sure the book has their correct telephone numbers and addresses in it.

Variation: Write the following on the chalkboard:

- a bicycle repair shop
- a toy store
- a pizza shop
- a stationery store

Direct children to the yellow pages to find the stores listed.

◆ Adding Up To $1.00

Group Activity

Here's an activity designed to teach students that money of different denominations can be used to create the same value. It also reinforces addition skills. To prepare for this activity, gather enough real coins for everyone in your class or duplicate the play money (page 110). Make sure the total of all the coins adds up to a dollar amount such as $4.00 or $10.00. As children come into the room, hand each a coin. Tell them to form a group with other children so that when that group combines its coins, they add up to exactly $1.00.

◆ Finding, Counting, And Cutting Things

Group Activity

This activity is an effective way to teach counting and classifying skills. Organize children into groups. Provide each group with safety scissors and an assortment of magazines. Write the following things on chalkboard:

7 pairs of pants	3 pieces of furniture	9 cars
5 pieces of jewelry	6 kinds of food	4 houses

Tell each group to select one of them from the chalkboard. Then have the group search through the magazines to find the designated number of pictures of each item. Share each group's results with the class.

Extender: Put a blank sheet of paper on each child's desk. Make sure they each have paste in addition to safety scissors. Have children use the pictures they cut out to create a collage.

◆ Find The Dictionary

Group Activity

Have children find dictionaries before they find words! Hide the entire pile of class dictionaries somewhere in the classroom. Attach the footsteps (page 109) to the floor in a path to the pile. At the pile, have a little sign that tells them what to do with the dictionaries.

◆ Familiar Shapes In The Classroom

Group Activity

Shapes are everywhere. Help children develop their visual skills by asking them to find shapes. Organize children into groups. Give each group one of the following shapes:

circle	triangle
square	rectangle

Have each group work together to locate objects in the room that are that shape.

Variation: Give the group an object. Tell the group to find objects that are the same size or smaller or larger than it.

◆ The Silent-Feelings Game

Group Activity

Here's a game that is perfect for the many students who love to act. Organize children into groups. Give each child a single-word emotion that can be expressed silently. Instruct them not to tell anyone else what the emotion is. Here are some emotions you can use:

joy	sadness	fear	surprise
anger	worry	embarrassment	confusion

Tell them to think about how they look when they feel that way. Have one child act out the emotion without words, while the other group members try to guess it.

Group Activity

Pantomime is a creative way for children to convey information silently. Combine pantomime with sports and you have a winning filler. Organize children into groups. Give each group a slip of paper with one of the following sports on it:

baseball	football	soccer
tennis	basketball	skiing
golf	ice skating	boxing
gymnastics	running	surfing

Allow two minutes for each group to plan their pantomime. Then invite each group to pantomime the sport for the rest of the class. If the class guesses the correct sport, the group gets a point. The group with the most points wins.

Variation: Give every child in each group a slip of paper with the name of a sport written on it. Tell children not to show their slips of paper to anyone else. Then invite each child to pantomime the sport in front of the group. The group gets a point if they can guess it. The group with the most points wins.

◆ Farm Or Jungle Animals

Group Activity

All children love animals. Here's a good way to help your students categorize them. Organize children into two groups. Place animals that live on a farm in the center of one group; place animals that live in the jungle in the center of the other group. The animals can be a cut-out pictures or plastic figures. Ask the children where they might find the animals that are in the center of their group. Once they have determined whether that is the farm or the jungle, have them brainstorm a list of other animals that are also found there. (If students are having trouble with the concept of jungle animals, substitute zoo animals.)

Extender: 1. Have children brainstorm information about the animals' habitat. Provide children with pictures and books about the habitat they are discussing.

2. Have the groups with farm animals work together to create a farm for their animals. Have the groups with jungle animals create their own jungle or zoo. Children can make the habitats from construction paper and cardboard.

Variation: Give each group objects representing the city and the country. The city object might be a skyscraper and the country object might be a barn. Have children brainstorm other things that are in the country, the city, or both.

Tell Me About That Stuffed Animal

Group Activity

Most young children spend hours playing with stuffed animals at home. Here's an opportunity for children to cuddle them in school. Organize children into groups. Place a stuffed animal in the center of each group. Ask children to look at and touch the animal. Have the group name it. Then have children pass the animal around. As each child holds the animal, have her tell the group something about it.

Extender: Have children write a group story about something that their stuffed animal has done.

It's In The Bag

Group Activity

Here is a great way to motivate children to describe things more precisely. Divide the class into small groups. Give every group a brown paper bag. Have children choose an object that fits in the bag. Then invite them to sit as a group on the floor. Have each group brainstorm words to describe the object in the bag.

Extender: Designate one child in each group to write down all the descriptive words the group members come up with. Have the groups take turns reading the descriptions of their bagged objects to the rest of the class. Can the other children guess what the objects are?

◆ Dropping It Into Water

Group Activity

Here's a filler that's great to use when you are studying water or mass. Organize children into groups. Fill several clear containers with water. Place those containers in pans to catch spills. Put one container in the center of each group. Provide pennies, rocks, paper clips, and other objects that will sink. Have each group count how long it takes for each object to sink to the bottom of the container. What objects take the longest? Help children to understand that the shape and weight of an object affects the speed at which it reaches the bottom.

◆ Float Or Sink?

Group Activity

Here is a scientific filler that will delight your students. Organize children into groups. Fill several clear containers with water. Place these containers in pans to catch spills. Put one container in the center of each group. Provide children with objects that will float and objects that will sink.

- Objects that will float: corks, balsa wood, sponges
- Objects that will sink: coins, paper clips, beans

Have children guess whether an object will float or sink. Then have them see if they are right.

◆ How Many?

Group Activity

Children love to estimate how many objects are in a
container. Why not start their day doing just that? Organize
children into groups. Fill a paper cup with small objects such
as paper clips or peanuts. Place a cup filled with objects on
the floor in the center of each group. Challenge groups to
estimate the number of objects in their cups. Ask children to
write their estimates on slips of paper. Then have each
group count the actual number of objects in the cup. Ask
children to compare their estimates with the actual number.

Extender: Have every group fill a cup with small objects.
Tell them to write down the number of objects they put in
the cups. Have groups exchange cups and estimate the
amount.

◆ Recycle This

Group Activity

Everybody's talking about recycling.
Here is a simple yet practical
introduction to this concept that
will also stimulate children's
imaginations. Organize children into
groups. Then tell each group to sit
in a circle on the floor. Give each
group a container that otherwise
would be thrown away. It might
be a yogurt container, a soup can,
or a cereal box. Ask children to
brainstorm other ways to use the
container.

Extender: Have children use the
container in the way they chose.

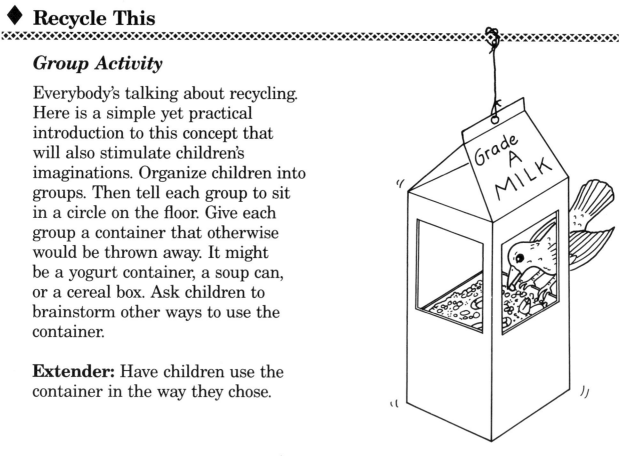

WALL STARTERS AND FILLERS

The walls and chalkboards of your classroom are great places for your students to learn things. The activities in this section require children to focus on these areas. Several will delight students by giving them the opportunity to write on the chalkboard. Group activities are indicated as such.

◆ Coded Information

All children love secret messages! Here's a code that's fun and easy for students to use. For this code, the first letter of the alphabet appears as the last letter (A = Z), the second letter of the alphabet appears as the second to last letter (B = Y), and so on. Write the code's solution on the chalkboard:

A	B	C	D	E	F	G	H	I	J	K	L	M
=	=	=	=	=	=	=	=	=	=	=	=	=
Z	Y	X	W	V	U	T	S	R	Q	P	O	N

N	O	P	Q	R	S	T	U	V	W	X	Y	Z
=	=	=	=	=	=	=	=	=	=	=	=	=
M	L	K	J	I	H	G	F	E	D	C	B	A

Then write a coded message for your students to crack. You can also give your students their new spelling words in the code.

Variation: Have children invent their own codes and write messages using them.

Extender: Write other messages during the day in the same code.

Keep The Color

Group Activity

This activity will make children more aware of their classroom environment. It is especially useful when you are teaching color recognition. Organize children into groups. Give each group a color. Allow three minutes for each group to walk around the room and search for things that are that color. Tell students not to remove any of the objects. Provide a space on the chalkboard for each group to list all the objects that they locate.

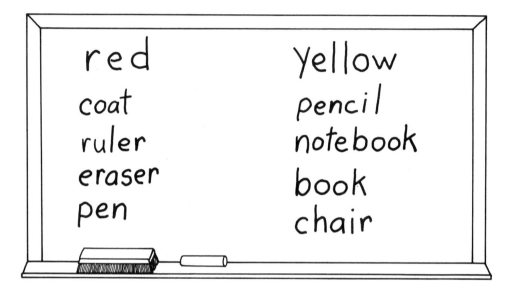

◆ Using Our Senses

The goal of this activity is to heighten students' awareness of the classroom environment and the usefulness of their senses. Write the following questions on the chalkboard:

• What can you see with your eyes?
• What can you hear with your ears?
• What can you smell with your nose?

Tell each student to answer one of the questions by listing all of the things she can detect using only that sense. Children need not leave their desks. Challenge students to do this for three minutes. Have children share the things that they sensed.

Extender: Create a class list for each sentence.

◆ Compound-Word Game

Children like making compound words and they'll love this game! Place a sheet of paper on each desk. Write the following words on the board:

ball	water	fall	snow	foot	man
mail	melon	sun	set	base	shine

Tell children to combine the words to form three real compound words. Then tell them to create three nonsense compound words. Ask a volunteer to read all of the compound words on his paper. Encourage the rest of the class to see if they can identify the nonsense words. For every nonsense word that passes as a real word, the volunteer gets one point. Give other students a chance to read their lists. The person with the most points wins.

Variation: 1. Have children create meanings for their nonsense compound words.
2. Organize children into groups to create their compound words. Give points to teams as opposed to individuals.

◆ Remembering Your Sense Of Taste

Here's a way to stimulate children's memories and their tastebuds as well. Create a list of all the foods the children ate yesterday. Write the list on the chalkboard. Then have students brainstorm which foods tasted sweet, sour, bitter, or salty.

◆ Let's Take A Poll

The results of this filler will delight children. Make a list of contemporary cartoon characters on the chalkboard. Have every child cast a vote for his favorite one. Choose a student to tally the votes. This child will put a mark next to the cartoon character each time it is selected.

Variation:
1. Poll children's feeling about television programs, spelling words, holidays, numbers, etc.
2. Have children create their own polls and take them in the classroom. Encourage children to publish their results.

◆ How Many Feet Long?

Group Activity

Here's an unusual measuring activity. Duplicate the footsteps (page 109). Organize children into four groups. Give each member of the group a footstep. Then have each group use the footsteps to "walk" across a wall of the room and find out how long it is. Have the group keep count of the number of footsteps required. Have the class discuss the measurement of each wall.

Extender:
1. Have the children measure the footprints against rulers. Using that information, ask them to calculate the actual length of each wall.
2. Discuss perimeter and area. Calculate the perimeter and area of the classroom using the footstep.

◆ Through The Hoop

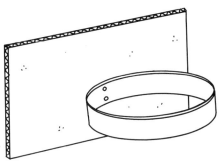 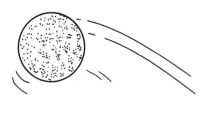

Try this one during the basketball season. Set up a few indoor basketball hoops. Place them at a height that will allow children to get the ball into the hoop with ease. The hoops can be purchased or made by attaching a cardboard cylinder to a piece of corrugated cardboard (see diagram). Provide a few balls of yarn, foam balls, or any type of balls that can be used indoors. Under each hoop, place a written assignment. As children enter the room, have them try to shoot the ball through the hoop. If they make a basket, they can take an assignment. If they don't make a basket after three tries, they also get to take an assignment.

◆ North, South, East And West

Here's an exciting way to teach children directional skills. Write a direction key such as the one below on the chalkboard. Read the words "North," "East," "South," and "West" aloud with children. then call out one of the words and ask all the students to stand up and face that direction. Repeat the activity until your class is familiar with each direction.

Variation: Choose a child to call out each direction.

North

West ← → East

South

◆ It's On The Map

Try this filler to help your students develop an awareness
of places in the United States. Hang a map of the United
States on a classroom wall. Assign children partners.
Give each pair a slip of paper containing the name of an
interesting place and a clue that will help them find it on
a map. The clue might be the state in which the place is
located or whether the place is located in the North, South,
East or West. Tell the pairs that they are going to visit the
places during imaginary vacations. Then have the pairs
locate their places on the map. Encourage children to help
each other.

Extender: 1. Take children to the library to research
information about their vacation spot.
2. Use the places as springboards for stories each
child will write about a vacation.

Variation: Hang a map of the world on a classroom wall. As
children enter, give them each a slip of a paper containing
the name of an action spot anywhere in the world.

◆ Let's Travel

Group Activity

Everyone dreams about going on a
trip. Organize children into groups.
Give each group two or three travel
brochures. Tell them to examine
each brochure and decide where
they would like to go on their
imaginary trips.

Extender: Have children
brainstorm things they would
do when they arrived at their
destination. Tell them to base those
activities on the information given
in the brochure.

◆ Giving Directions

Group Activity

Familiarity with the school building is a must for this filler. Organize children into groups. On the chalkboard, write the directions for getting from the front door of the school to the classroom. Ask a volunteer to read the directions. Explain to children that they followed this path to get to the classroom. Assign each group a place in the school. Ask each group to write down the directions that would lead students from their room to that place.

Variation: Present each group with a simple map showing the route from the front door of the school to the classroom. Then have them create a map of the route one would take to get from the classroom to the assigned spot.

Extender: Have the class follow each group's directions to the locations in the building. If the directions are inaccurate, ask the groups to alter them.

◆ It's An Emergency

It's always of value to draw children's attention to emergency telephone numbers. Write the local emergency numbers on the chalkboard. Discuss the appropriate times to use each number.

Extender: Give children time to memorize the numbers. Ask each child to work with the classmate seated next to her. Tell one of the students to name a type of emergency. Then have the other recite the appropriate number to call without looking at the chalkboard.

◆ Make A Mural

Group Activity

Did you ever consider starting the day with a group art activity? Try this one. Hang mural paper on the wall. Then write one of these titles on the paper.

• The Silliest Animals Ever Seen

• Things You Find In The City

• The Shapes We Know

• Creatures From Another Planet

Provide markers, crayons, or paints. Delight children by inviting them to create pictures that relate to the title. This activity can also be used as a filler. It's great for children who complete their assignments before the majority of the class.

Extender: Provide an array of materials to be added to the mural such as magazine pictures, yarn and sequins.

◆ The Analogy Game

Children love to complete analogies. Organize children into teams. Write a few simple analogies on the chalkboard. Give each team three minutes to complete the analogies. Here are some analogies you can use:

• Apple is to red as sun is to _____. (yellow)

• Finger is to hand as toe is to _____. (foot)

• On is to off as big is to _____. (little)

Give each team a point for every answer they get right.

Extender: Have children create their own analogies.

◆ Read Those Words Between My Fingers

This activity is useful to reinforce or introduce phonics skills. Duplicate the hands (page 108). On each hand, write a vocabulary, spelling, or sight word, or a word that stresses a particular phonics skill. Hang the hands on the classroom walls. As children enter the room, give them each one of the words that is on the wall. You can do this verbally or by giving them each a hand that matches one on the wall. Tell children to find the same word and to stand by it. Then have children read their words aloud.

Variation: Try this with numbers facts too.

◆ That's My Number

Group Activity

Organize children into groups by giving each child in a particular group the same number. Hang large sheets of newsprint on the walls around the room. Hang one sheet for each group and put that group's number on it. Tell the children to find the sheet that has their number on it. Then have each group brainstorm facts about that number. Circulate around the room checking to make sure the number facts are all correct.

Variation: Have each group brainstorm number facts that include their number in the fact. For example, if their number was four, they could list any of the following number facts:

$$4+1=5 \qquad 3+1=4 \qquad 4\times2=8 \qquad 5-1=4$$

◆ Pair Tongue Twisters

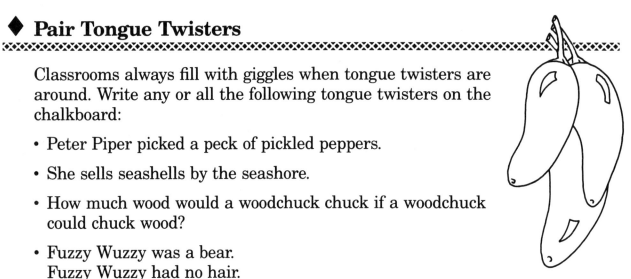

Classrooms always fill with giggles when tongue twisters are around. Write any or all the following tongue twisters on the chalkboard:

• Peter Piper picked a peck of pickled peppers.

• She sells seashells by the seashore.

• How much wood would a woodchuck chuck if a woodchuck could chuck wood?

• Fuzzy Wuzzy was a bear.
  Fuzzy Wuzzy had no hair.
  Fuzzy Wuzzy wasn't fuzzy.
  Was he?

Organize children into pairs. Then have children say the tongue twisters for each other or in unison.

Variation: Have children time one another to see who can say each tongue twister the fastest.

◆ Sentence Search

Watch your students smile as they do this activity. Write a sentence on the chalkboard. Then write single words from the sentence on small strips of paper. Put a different word on each child's desk. Ask children to locate other students who have words that will complete their sentences. (Eventually the sentence will be formed several times by several groups.) Then ask children to read the sentence aloud together.

Variation: Organize children into groups. Each child in the group must have a different word from the sentence. Ask each group to form new sentences by using all or some of the words in a different order.

◆ Category Game

Group Activity

Get any cobwebs out of your students' minds with this lively activity. Organize children into groups. Write a list of categories on the chalkboard. Have each group choose one category and brainstorm the things that belong in it. Choose one child in every group to be the scribe. Ask that child to write the group's ideas on a designated spot on the chalkboard. Possible categories include:

- Things that are red
- Things that you find in school
- Things that you can eat
- Things that are made of wood

If children are having difficulty, tell them to look around the room for ideas.

Variation: 1. This activity can be done with categories relating to phonics. Possible activities include:

- Words that rhyme with *bat*
- Words that begin with *th*
- Words that end in *tion*
- Words with the short *a* sound in them

2. This activity can also be done with number facts. Possible categories include:

- Even numbers
- Odd numbers between 50 and 100
- Numbers that can be added to other numbers to equal 7
- Numbers that can be multiplied by other numbers to equal 12

◆ Count It Out

Do your students realize how many of the same thing can be found in your classroom? Send your students searching for specific objects and they will learn exactly how many books, blocks, and desks there are in your room. Write the names of the objects to be found on the chalkboard. For example:

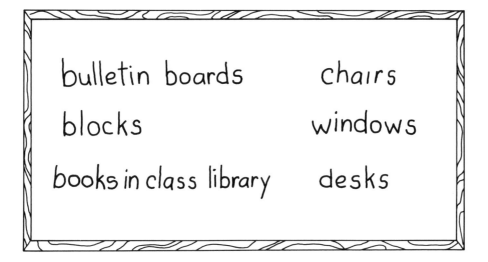

bulletin boards   chairs

blocks   windows

books in class library   desks

Have each child choose a partner. Assign each pair of students an object listed on the chalkboard. Challenge them to count how many of that object are in the classroom. Be sure to assign more than one pair of students to count each object. Have each pair write their results next to the name of the object on the chalkboard. Have children compare their results.

Extender: If children have different answers, ask them to work together to recount the objects.

◆ Noting The Change On The Wall

This activity will teach your students to pay attention to the smallest of details. Change a bulletin board or something on one of the walls in the classroom. As children enter the room, tell them that something is different, but do not tell them what it is. When all children have had ample time to look around the room, ask them to tell you what has changed.

◆ It's A Rainbow

Everyone loves a rainbow! On poster board, draw the seven strips of a rainbow. Write the names of each color in the rainbow. Hang the poster on a wall. Cut pieces of paper that are the seven colors of the rainbow. Hide them in the classroom. Be sure to hide enough pieces so that everyone will be able to find at least one. As children enter, assign every child a color. Ask each of them to search for a piece of paper that is that color. When children find the colors, tell them to paste the colors onto the strips of the rainbow.

Variation: 1. Fill in one color of the rainbow each day, for seven days.
2. Have each child look for a piece of paper that has his color on it.

Extender: Make the project last for a few days by making the rainbow very big and hiding new pieces of paper each day.

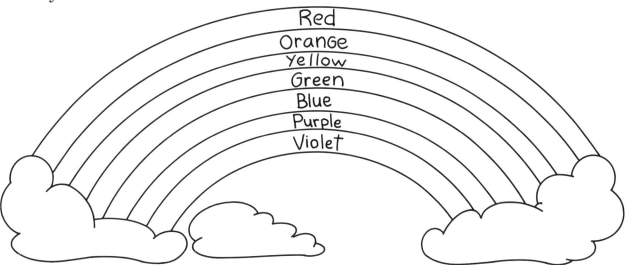

◆ It's In The Bag

This activity is a lot like going to the movies because it requires tickets. Duplicate the tickets (page 107). On each ticket, write the name of a classroom center. Hang a bag or a large envelope on the wall and put the tickets in it. As children arrive, have them pick a ticket from the bag. Tell them to proceed to the centers on their tickets.

◆ Indoor, Outdoor, And Both

Group Activity

Here's a filler that requires children to use their classification skills. Organize children into four groups. On the chalkboard, write the following heading four times so that each group has their own.

- Indoors
- Outdoors
- Both

Tell the groups that they have four minutes to brainstorm games that can be played indoors, outdoors, and both. Have each group write their responses under the correct heading on the chalkboard. Then tell the groups they have three minutes to brainstorm which games on their lists are *Noisy* and which games are *Quiet*. Have children write *Noisy* or *Quiet* next to each game.

Extender: Give each group a criterion for choosing a game. For example, you might say: "What game can only be played outdoors and is quiet?" Tell groups to use their lists to determine their answers.

◆ Syllable Bag

Here's a chance to individualize the learning of syllables. Hang three manila envelopes on the wall. Write the numbers *1*, *2*, and *3* on the separate envelopes. As each child enters the room, direct her to one of the envelopes and ask her to write a word that has that number of syllables on a slip of paper. Tell her to put the slip of paper in the envelope. Be sure to match the child's skill level to the number of syllables in the word you give her.

SPECIAL-DAY STARTERS AND FILLERS

AT-THE-DOOR STARTERS AND FILLERS

Want a special moment for a special day? Choose any of these very short activities to start your students' days. The Holiday and Seasonal Starters appear in chronological order with the exception of those activities that are adaptable to a variety of holidays or seasons.

♥ Special Seats

It's the first day of school. Everyone is wondering where they will sit. As children arrive, give them name tags to put on their desks. Then invite them to use crayons to decorate their tags.

♥ Christopher Columbus's Voyage

Bon Voyage! As children arrive ask them to imagine that they are sailing across the ocean with Christopher Columbus. Invite children to tell you things they might see, feel, taste, touch, or hear on that voyage.

♥ Witches Walk-In

It's Halloween and the goblins are stirring. Invite each of your students to enter the room in a witch-like manner. Or perhaps they would like to float in like ghosts.

♥ March Like A Soldier

It's Veteran's Day! Ask everyone to march like soldiers into the classroom with their shoulders back, heads held high, and in a straight line.

Variation: This starter works well for Memorial Day too.

♥ Who's Running For Office?

Develop an awareness of Election Day among your students. Just prior to Election Day, as homework, ask your students to find out who is running for office. Let them know you will be asking them about the election. As students arrive the next day, ask them to whisper the name of a candidate.

Variation: Ask children to find out which offices candidates will be running for. Then ask them to recall what they learned at home the evening before.

♥ You Are A Turkey

Everyone thinks about turkeys when Thanksgiving is near. As children arrive, ask them to act like turkeys as they enter the classroom.

♥ December Delights

All children look forward to December. They are all hoping the holidays will bring them something special. Share a special moment by asking children to whisper to you the name of the special thing they want. Then when everyone has arrived tell them your special wish.

♥ Name That President

It's President's Day. When students are lined up to enter the classroom, whisper this sentence to the first child: "President's Day celebrates Abraham Lincoln's and George Washington's birthdays." Then have the first child whisper the sentence to the second child and so on. After a child tells the next child, she can enter the room. Tell the last child to repeat the sentence aloud. If the sentence is jumbled, tell everyone what the actual sentence was. If the chain of whispers gets broken, start the activity again with the same sentence.

♥ St. Patrick's Day Parade

Have children make their own St. Patrick's Day Parade. Play a tape or record of Irish music. Then invite all of your students to line up and march into the classroom.

♥ How This Holiday Makes Me Feel

This starter allows you to share a special moment with each student. Before each child enters the room, have him share one of his thoughts about the upcoming holiday with you by whispering it in your ear.

❄ Autumn Leaves

Fill your room with a sign of the season. In fall, invite the children to bring their favorite autumn leaves to school on the following morning. As children enter the next day, have them show you their leaves and name all the colors in them.

Extender: Ask students to place their leaves in a basket provided. This collection can be used later as a springboard for writing, science, etc.

Note: Children who are allergic to leaves should not be involved in this activity.

❄ Warming Up In Winter

In winter, everyone puts on their warmest clothing. Ask children to name articles of clothing that they put on to keep warm in the winter.

❄ It's Cold In The Winter

Winter is the coldest season. Ask each student to name something that is cold as she enters the room.

❄ Spring Flowers

Everyone loves spring flowers. In spring, invite each child to bring a flower to school on the following morning. As children enter the next day, have them show you their flowers and name all the colors in them. Then create a class bouquet for all to see.

Extender: Use the bouquet as a springboard for drawing or writing exercises.

Note: Children who are allergic to flowers should not be involved in this activity.

❄ Seasonal Feelings

Use this activity on the first day of each season. Let children share their feelings about the season at the start the day. As they enter the room, ask them to tell you how the season makes them feel.

❄ Seasonal Sports

People usually ski in the winter and swim outdoors in the summer. Help children associate sports with seasons. As the new season begins, ask each child to think of a sport that is often done at that time of year. Then have them write the sports on the chalkboard before they take their seats.

🎈 Birthday Wishes

Here's a way to make a child feel very special on his birthday. Ask the birthday child to arrive a little early. Then ask that child to stand at the door to welcome his classmates to class. Encourage the other students to express their birthday wishes before they enter the room.

✤ Trip Time

Help children relive a class trip with this starter! Greet each child with the question: "What was your favorite time during the class trip yesterday?" Encourage children to whisper their responses.

DESKTOP STARTERS AND FILLERS

These entertaining activities are designed to take place at each child's desk. The Holiday and Seasonal Starters and Fillers appear in chronological order with the exception of those activities that are adaptable to a variety of holidays or seasons.

♥ It's My Desk

Everyone likes their workspace to reflect their personality. Let children create special name tags for their desks. Children will need some crayons, markers, safety scissors, and construction paper. Invite children to design name tags that are as unique as they are.

♥ Welcome-To-School Maze

School has just begun. Young children often feel that finding their way to and around school is like a maze. Duplicate the Welcome-To-School Maze (page 77), pass it out, and let students find their way through it. Then discuss the confusion students may feel on the first days of school.

Note: The answer key is on page 112.

Welcome To School

Help the student find his way to school.

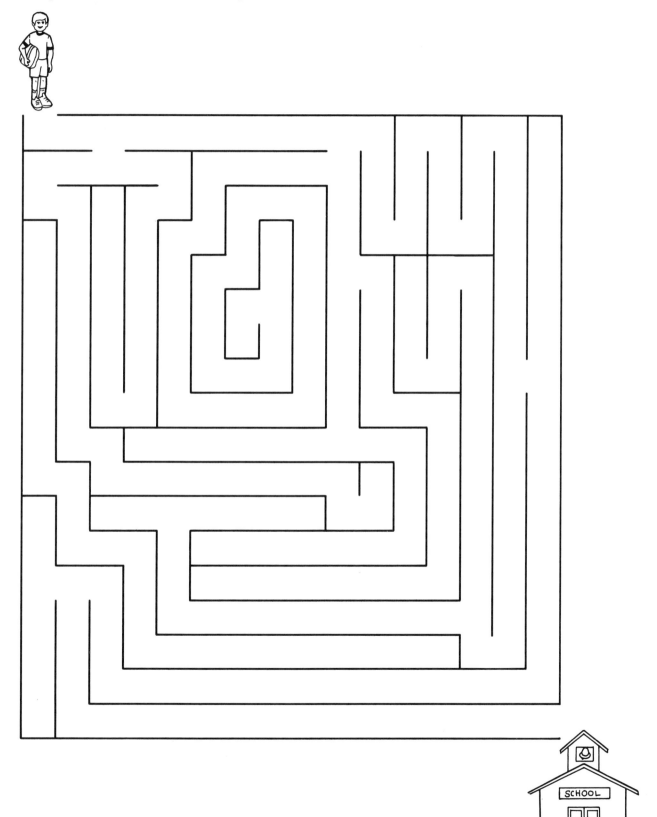

♥ School Supply Word-Search Puzzle

The beginning of school means new school supplies. Help children get acquainted with all the supplies they'll be using throughout the year with this special activity. Duplicate the School Supply Word-Search Puzzle (page 79). Give one to each student to solve.

Extender: Once they've completed the puzzle, discuss how many of each item they will need.

Note: The answer key is on page 112.

♥ Happy Halloween Bookmarks

There are so many books with Halloween as a theme. Why not have children make Halloween bookmarks? Give each student a six-inch by three-inch strip of orange construction paper and a black crayon or marker. Encourage everyone to draw witches, ghosts, and jack-o-lanterns on the bookmarks.

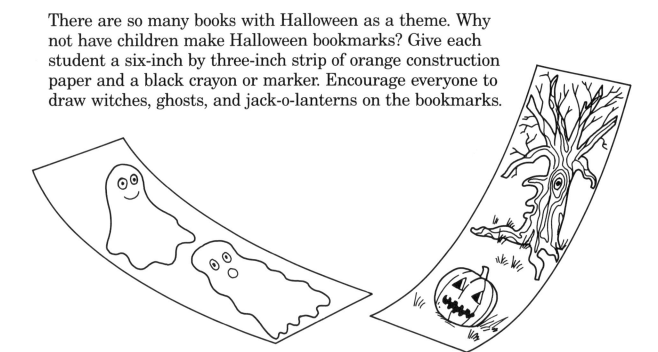

♥ Trick Or Treat

It's Halloween. Let children anticipate the treats they will get with this fun activity. Provide each child with a piece of white paper cut into the shape of ghost. Tell children that this ghost is about to go trick or treating. Tell each child to write a list on the ghost of all the treats that she thinks the ghost will get.

Searching For School Supplies

Can you find all of these hidden words in the puzzle? Circle each one.

NOTEBOOKS, PENS, CRAYONS, STAPLER, STAPLES, PENCILS, BOOKS, BOOK COVERS, ERASERS, GLUE, PAPER, DICTIONARY, LOOSELEAF, SCISSORS, RULER

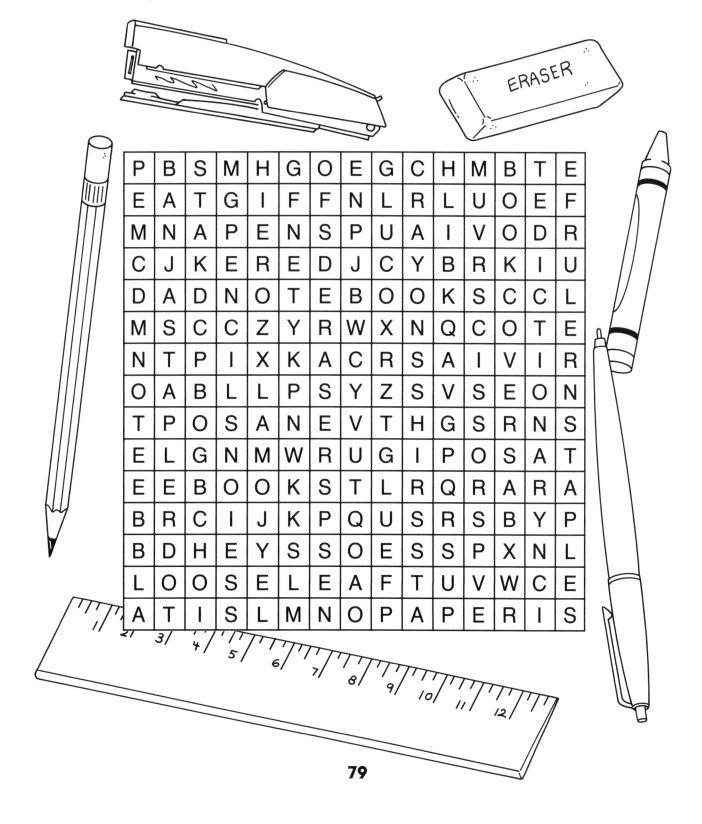

P	B	S	M	H	G	O	E	G	C	H	M	B	T	E
E	A	T	G	I	F	F	N	L	R	L	U	O	E	F
M	N	A	P	E	N	S	P	U	A	I	V	O	D	R
C	J	K	E	R	E	D	J	C	Y	B	R	K	I	U
D	A	D	N	O	T	E	B	O	O	K	S	C	C	L
M	S	C	C	Z	Y	R	W	X	N	Q	C	O	T	E
N	T	P	I	X	K	A	C	R	S	A	I	V	I	R
O	A	B	L	L	P	S	Y	Z	S	V	S	E	O	N
T	P	O	S	A	N	E	V	T	H	G	S	R	N	S
E	L	G	N	M	W	R	U	G	I	P	O	S	A	T
E	E	B	O	O	K	S	T	L	R	Q	R	A	R	A
B	R	C	I	J	K	P	Q	U	S	R	S	B	Y	P
B	D	H	E	Y	S	S	O	E	S	S	P	X	N	L
L	O	O	S	E	L	E	A	F	T	U	V	W	C	E
A	T	I	S	L	M	N	O	P	A	P	E	R	I	S

♥ Voting-Day Maze

Everyone should vote. Duplicate the Voting-Day Maze (page 81). Give a copy to every student. Invite children to complete the maze by getting the voter to the voting booth. Then you might send home the completed maze to parents as a reminder.

Note: The answer key is on page 112.

♥ A Thankful Turkey

This filler makes a lovely Thanksgiving decoration. Get a pumpkin (or a large squash) to use as the body of a turkey. Cut out a turkey head from paper. Attach the head to the pumpkin. Then cut out pieces of colored construction paper in the shape of turkey feathers. As each child enters the room, give him a turkey feather. Ask each child to write something for which he is grateful on the feather. Then attach all the feathers to the pumpkin. Voilà you have a Thankful Turkey. Display the turkey for the class to enjoy.

Extender: Have children share the things for which they are grateful with the class.

Vote Today

Find the correct path from home to the voting booth.

♥ Thanksgiving Word-Search Puzzle

Most people think of the same things when they hear the word "Thanksgiving." Give your students the opportunity to find those things with this great quiet-time activity. Duplicate the Thanksgiving Word-Search Puzzle (page 83) and distribute a copy to each student in your class. See if anyone can find all the hidden words.

Note: The answer key is on page 112.

♥ December Holiday Associations

In December, bring some holiday "gifts" into the classroom. Wrap empty boxes in white paper and put bows on them. Organize children into groups and give each group a box. Have each group write all the words that remind them of the holiday season on the box.

Variation: 1. Wrap one large box for the class. Invite children to take turns writing words that remind them of the holiday season on the box. If you are planning to give out little holiday presents, you might put them inside this class box.
    2. Use this activity for any holiday associated with gift-giving. Those holidays include: Mother's Day, Father's Day, and Valentine's Day.

Name _____

Thanksgiving Word-Search Puzzle

Can you find all of these hidden words in the puzzle? Circle each one.

TURKEY, INDIAN CORN, MASSACHUSETTS, PILGRIMS, AUTUMN, PUMPKIN PIE, INDIANS, PLYMOUTH, HAYSTACKS, HARVEST, UNITED STATES, STUFFING

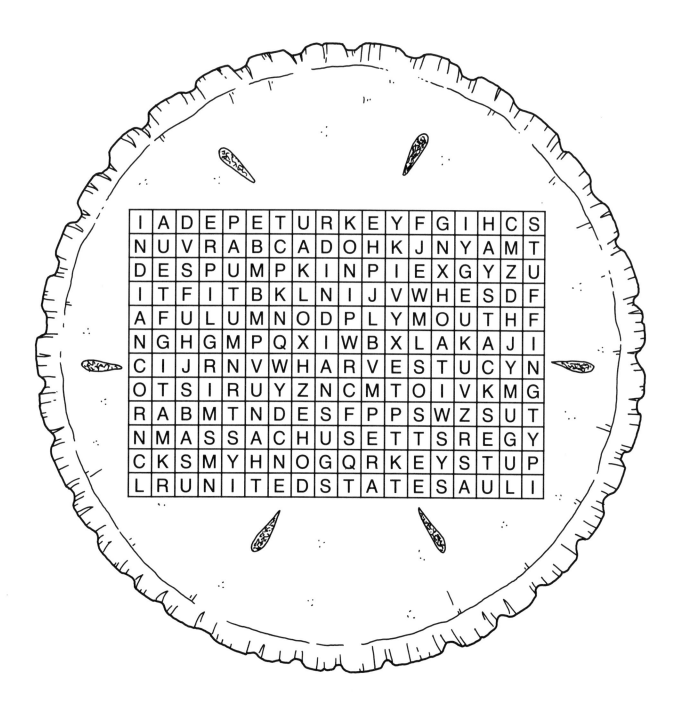

I	A	D	E	P	E	T	U	R	K	E	Y	F	G	I	H	C	S
N	U	V	R	A	B	C	A	D	O	H	K	J	N	Y	A	M	T
D	E	S	P	U	M	P	K	I	N	P	I	E	X	G	Y	Z	U
I	T	F	I	T	B	K	L	N	I	J	V	W	H	E	S	D	F
A	F	U	L	U	M	N	O	D	P	L	Y	M	O	U	T	H	F
N	G	H	G	M	P	Q	X	I	W	B	X	L	A	K	A	J	I
C	I	J	R	N	V	W	H	A	R	V	E	S	T	U	C	Y	N
O	T	S	I	R	U	Y	Z	N	C	M	T	O	I	V	K	M	G
R	A	B	M	T	N	D	E	S	F	P	P	S	W	Z	S	U	T
N	M	A	S	S	A	C	H	U	S	E	T	T	S	R	E	G	Y
C	K	S	M	Y	H	N	O	G	Q	R	K	E	Y	S	T	U	P
L	R	U	N	I	T	E	D	S	T	A	T	E	S	A	U	L	I

♥ Valentines For The Classroom

Here's a new twist on valentines. Invite children to create valentine cards for objects in the room that they really appreciate. For example, a child might make a card for the pencil sharpener because it keeps a point on her pencil. Whatever the object, the child should express her appreciation to it in the card.

To
My pencil sharpener

Roses are red
Violets are blue
My pencils are nice and sharp
I owe it all to you!
Love - Carrie

♥ Find The Leprechauns

St. Patrick's Day has arrived. Duplicate the Find-The-Leprechauns activity sheet (page 85). Give one to all students and tell them to see how many leprechauns they can find hidden in the picture. Can anyone find all 15?

Find The Leprechauns

Can you find the fifteen Leprechauns hidden in this picture?
Circle each one.

♥ Thoughts About Mom Or Dad

Moms are very special people. Use this filler as a way for children to express how very special their moms are. Place a sheet of paper on each desk. Tell students to write the word *MOM* vertically on it (as shown above). Then have each child add the word (or words) that best describes his mother. Those words must begin with *M*, *O*, and *M*. Have students add artwork if they wish. Then tell them to take the finished products home to their moms.

Variation: Have children use the word *Dad* in the same manner on Father's Day.

Note: If a child in the classroom does not have a mom or dad be sure to handle this activity with great sensitivity.

♥ Color-The-Flag Puzzle

Flag Day is June 14. Why not celebrate with your students. Duplicate the Color-The-Flag Puzzle (page 87). Distribute one to each child in the class along with a red, white, and blue crayon. Tell them to color each shape the color that is indicated. They will be delighted by the picture that emerges.

Color-The-Flag Puzzle

Use the code to color the spaces in the puzzle below.

■ = blue   ○ = red   ☆ = white

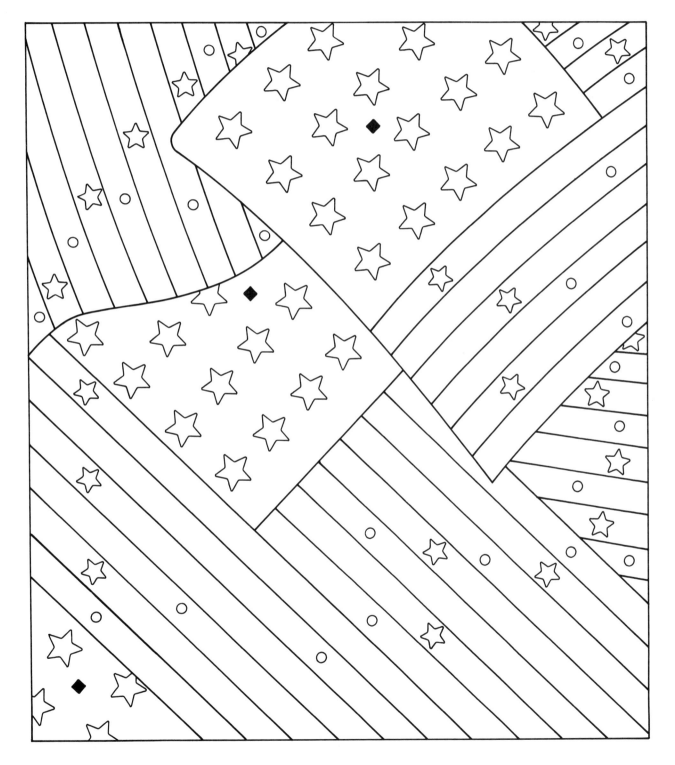

What did you find? _____

♥ A Holiday Color

Most people associate color or colors with holidays. For example, mention Valentine's Day and they will think of red or pink. On or just before a holiday, give each child a piece of paper that is the color typically associated with that holiday. (For those holidays that have more than one color associated with them, give children smaller pieces of multiple colors.) Ask children to use the paper to create something about the holiday. Tell children they can use pens, markers, crayons, safety scissors, glue and anything else they have at their desk. Make sure you let them know how long they have to work on their creations.

Extender: Using their creations, make a display about the holiday.

♥ Name The Holiday By The Tune

Play a tape or record of music associated with an upcoming holiday. Ask children to name the holiday. Then have children brainstorm other songs that are about that holiday or that remind them of it.

♥ Holiday Trivia Box

Everyone loves trivia. Why not create your own Holiday Trivia Box. Place an index card on each child's desk. After children enter the room, have them brainstorm information about the upcoming holiday. Write their responses on the chalkboard. Then have children choose a fact they liked and write it on the index card along with the holiday's name. Collect all the cards and place them in the box.

Extender: Repeat the same activity for each holiday. Soon you will have your box filled with interesting facts about all the different holidays. By June, you'll be ready to have a Holiday Trivia Game! Here's how to play:

Choose one child to pick a holiday fact from the Holiday Trivia Box. Ask him to read the fact aloud, but not the name of the holiday. See if the rest of class can guess the holiday. If no one guesses correctly, reveal the answer. Then select another card, and so on.

♥ Holiday Songs

Bring a little music into the classroom with this special activity. As children enter the room, have a tape or record of a familiar holiday song playing. On the chalkboard, write the words to the song. Ask the children to take their seats, follow the words on the board, and sing along with the music if they wish.

♥ Hidden Holiday Symbols

Here's something to use again and again during the school year. Duplicate the Hidden-Picture Notepaper (page 91). At each holiday, distribute a copy to every student. Tell children to color in only the symbol for that holiday. In the center of the notepaper, have the children write the name of the holiday. If they wish they can turn the notepaper into a holiday card for someone special.

Variation: Have students use the notepaper to write holiday stories and poems, and to draw holiday pictures.

Extender: Tell children to write the various ways that people celebrate the holiday in the center of their notepaper.

♥ Create A Holiday

Here's a filler that gives students the opportunity to create their own holidays! Place a sheet of paper on each desk. Ask children to think of someone famous, who does not have a holiday named after him or her. Then ask children to create their own holidays by answering the following questions:

1. Who is the person?
2. What is the date of the holiday to honor them?
3. What is the name of the holiday?
4. In what way will the country celebrate the holiday?

(Tell students that possible methods of celebration include parades, fireworks, and gift-giving.)

Variation: Have children create a holiday for themselves. Ask them to write down all the reasons they should have their own personal holiday, the date the holiday should be, and how the country should celebrate it.

Extender: Have children write an explanation of why this holiday should be celebrated.

❄ Finding Colors In Autumn Leaves

Get your students into the season with this fall filler. Gather autumn leaves that all have more than one color in them. Give each student a leaf, a sheet of paper with the outline of a leaf on it (see art above), and fall-color crayons. Ask children to study the colors of their leaves. Then have them each color in the paper leaf using the colors.

Variation: Provide each child with a blank sheet of drawing paper (instead of one with the outline of a leaf on it). Ask children to trace the shape of their leaves and then to color them.

❄ Winter White

Children love to read stories that have a lot of alliteration. So why not invite children to create their own alliterative descriptions of winter? To get their vocabularies activated, give students these examples: wonderous winter white, slippery slush sliding, snickering snowflakes, and wild winds whirling. After everyone is done, allow time for volunteers to share their creations with the class.

❄ Create A Season

This filler will increase students' awareness of the differences between the seasons. Duplicate the nature scene (page 94). As each season begins, place a copy of the scene on each child's desk. Make sure that every child has markers or crayons. Tell students to color in the picture to reflect the new season. Encourage them to write captions about the season below their pictures.

Extender: Create a seasonal bulletin board. Display the children's pictures of one season. Then when new pictures are completed, have children compare them to the old pictures and note the differences.

❀ Birthday Candles

Place a sheet of construction paper with the outline of a cake on it on the birthday child's desk. Ask other children to each draw a candle and to write a birthday message inside it. Then ask the children to hand deliver the candles to the birthday person. The birthday child can tape the candles onto the cake.

Create A Season

Use crayons to color the picture the colors of the season. Then write a sentence about the season.

Bring some birthday cheer into your classroom with this activity. At the beginning of the school year, decorate a shoe box to be used as the Birthday Box. Bring out the box each time a child celebrates a birthday. Duplicate the stationery (page 91) for each child's birthday. On the chalkboard, write the name of the child who is celebrating his birthday. Also write the actual day and date of his birthday. Tell students to each write a brief message for the birthday child on the stationery. (Remind children to sign their messages.) Then have them place the messages in the Birthday Box. Place the Birthday Box on the birthday child's desk so that he can read all the messages. Be sure to plan a day for each child who has a birthday when school is not in session to receive the Birthday Box.

Variation: When you write the birthday child's name on the chalkboard, write the year of his birth in addition to the day and date. Subtract that year from the current year to determine the child's age.

Extender: Have the birthday child read the messages aloud or let the children who created them read them to the birthday child and the whole class.

✣ Remember A Class Trip

While on a class trip, gather mementos. If it was a nature walk, for example, you might bring back small specimens of the different plants and rocks you noticed. Divide children into groups. Give a trip memento to each group. Ask each group to tell about their item. How and why does it remind them of their trip?

✣ Preparing Trip Tags

Before each trip, have children create name tags. Pass out index cards and ask students to draw the shape of the place you'll be visiting. On a museum trip, you might ask them to draw the shape of the building. A zoo trip might call for an animal shape. Ask children to use a pencil to write their name and the school name inside the shape. Encourage children to use their best handwriting. Then have children trace over their letters with a colored marker, cut out the shape and pin onto their clothing.

✣ Talking About Trip Behavior

Here's an amusing activity that will help guarantee that your students behave well on school outings. Have children brainstorm appropriate trip behavior. After the first child suggests a proper way to behave, have the second child repeat the first idea and add an idea of her own. Then have a third child repeat the first and second ideas before adding his own.

These starters and fillers are group activities. The Holiday and Seasonal Starters and Fillers appear in chronological order with exception of those activities that are adaptable to a variety of holidays or seasons.

♥ Halloween Ghosts Speak Out

Here's a spooky activity! Before children arrive, draw one, two, or three ghosts on the chalkboard. From the mouth of each ghost, draw a gigantic cartoon speech bubble. As children arrive, ask them to write a short message from the ghost in a bubble. Make sure the bubble is large enough for several children to write inside.

♥ Columbus Sailed Across The Seas

Group Activity

Organize the children into groups. Pose the following question: What problems do you think Columbus faced when he was at sea? Have each group brainstorm a list of problems.

Extender: Have the groups think of solutions for each problem.

♥ Have A Safe Halloween

Group Activity

A safe Halloween is a concern of every adult. Here's a way to orient children towards safe trick or treating. Organize the children into groups. Tell each group to brainstorm ways to make trick or treating a safe activity. Then have all of the groups share their ideas with each other.

♥ A Veteran's Day Or Memorial Day Parade

Group Activity

Play a tape or record of a military march. As children enter the room, have them parade around the room in time to the rhythm. If you have any band instruments available, give them to the children to use in the parade.

♥ A Turkey Tale

Group Activity

Get everyone laughing with this Thanksgiving activity. Have children gather around you for a "A Turkey Tale." You can start the tale with these sentences: "It is Thanksgiving. The turkeys are preparing their Thanksgiving feast. 'What shall we serve this year?' gobbled Thaddeus Turkey." Invite children to add to your story. As each child adds one idea, encourage another volunteer to continue the story in a humorous vein.

Variation: Have younger children simply name the foods that the turkeys will eat.

♥ The Bunny Hop

Group Activity

It's almost Easter. Use this filler when children are getting restless. Invite children to get in a line and do the Bunny Hop.

♥ Happy Mother's Or Father's Day

Group Activity

Organize children into groups. For three minutes, have them brainstorm all the things that moms do that are special. Then write everyone's ideas on the chalkboard.

Variation: For Father's Day, have children brainstorm the special things that fathers do.

Note: If a child in the classroom does not have a mom or dad be sure to handle this activity with great sensitivity.

❄ Autumn Leaf Count

Group Activity

Children love autumn leaves. Ask children to bring some leaves to school on a designated day. As children arrive, have them create a pile of leaves on the classroom floor. Once the pile is complete, ask students to guess the number of leaves in the pile. Then count the leaves and compare the actual number with the predictions.

Note: Check to make certain no children are allergic to leaves before starting this activity.

❄ What Is Snow?

Group Activity

You'll need a snowy day for this activity. Organize children into groups. Give each group a cup of snow that you have collected from outside. Have children observe that the snow turns into water. Then have children brainstorm why this might happen. (If children are having difficulty concluding that heat turns snow into water, have them move their cups near the radiator to accelerate the melting process.)

❄ Words Of The Season

Group Activity

Organize children into groups. Give each group two minutes to brainstorm as many words as they can associated with the season that is just beginning. Ask one member of the group to be the scribe. Then have each group read their list aloud.

❄ Comparing Spring Flowers

Group Activity

Bring in a bouquet of garden flowers to your classroom. If a bouquet is unavailable, bring in pictures from a spring flower catalog. Organize children into groups. Give each group flowers. Have them compare the look and smell of the flowers.

Variation: Ask the groups to separate the flowers by color. Have them put all the red flowers together, all the yellow flowers together, and so on.

Note: Children who are allergic to flowers should not be involved in this activity.

🎈 It's Your Birthday

Group Activity

When it's a student's birthday, have the child choose a circle, a square, a rectangle, or a circle. Then have the rest of the class form that shape by holding hands. Tell the birthday child to stand in the middle of the shape while her classmates sing "Happy Birthday."

♀ Sharing Birthday Memories

Group Activity

This filler works especially well when children have warm feelings for one another. Have children sit in a circle on the floor. Beginning with the birthday child, encourage each student to share a favorite birthday memory.

✤ Memories From A Class Trip

Group Activity

Organize mementos that you have gathered from class trips in the following way: Place four things from one trip and one thing from another trip together. Organize children into groups. Give each group five items. Have them determine which one comes from a different place than the others. Then ask the children to name the places the mementos are from.

✤ Trip Checklist

Are all of your students prepared for the class trip? Use this activity to make sure. Write the following checklist on the board. Prior to departing, review the list and have a volunteer check off each question as you read it.

1. Do you know which adult you should stay with on the trip?
2. Do you know who your partner is?
3. Do you know the bus safety rules?
4. Do you have a name tag? (If these are used in your school.)
5. Do you have your lunch? (If it is a full-day trip.)
6. Do you have your trip money? (If this is permitted in your school.)

WALL STARTERS AND FILLERS

Classroom excitement always builds on special days. Add to
the specialness of the day with one of these activities that
makes use of a wall or the chalkboard. The Holiday and
Seasonal Starters and Fillers appear in chronological order
with the exception of those activities that are adaptable to a
variety of holidays or seasons.

♥ Welcoming Words

It's the first day of school. Everyone is welcoming the
children to the school. As children arrive, give them
chalk. Then invite them to write some welcoming words
of their own.

♥ Let's Vote

Demonstrate the power of voting with this simple activity.
Give children the opportunity to vote for the morning activity
they would like to do first. List all the possible activities on
the chalkboard, for example:

Reading
Spelling
Math
Social Studies

(cont.)

Explain to students that the activity that receives the most votes will be the first activity they do. Using a show of hands, take a class vote. Record the number of votes each activity receives on the chalkboard. Then go to it!

Extender: Have children vote by secret ballot. Explain the reasons for a secret ballot. Discuss with children why their parents vote privately. If time permits, explain the concept of *majority rules*.

♥ A Pattern Of Hearts

Here's a *lovely* Valentine's activity. Cut hearts of many different sizes out of construction paper—one for each child in the class. Hang a large sheet of mural paper on the wall. On it, trace outlines of all the hearts. Put a heart and some crayons on every desk. Tell each child to decorate his heart and to write his name on it. Then have the child locate his heart's outline on the mural paper and attach the heart he colored to it. When the activity is over, you'll have a lively wall decoration.

Variation: Have children use their own hearts to create outlines on the mural paper.

♥ President's Skills

It's President's Day. Write "President" on the chalkboard. As children enter the classroom ask them to think of the kinds of skills a President must have to do the job. Ask each child to write her idea or ideas on the board. Discuss these ideas.

♥ Predict The Holiday Story

Place a holiday book on the chalk ledge. Ask children to look at the cover and the title and think about what the book will be about. Ask them to write a word or words that tell on the chalkboard. Later, discuss these ideas and then read the story.

♥ Name That Holiday

Children really enjoy this holiday activity. Create a short list of facts about a holiday. Write it on the chalkboard. Once all the children are seated, have them guess the holiday. Once they have determined the holiday, encourage children to add more facts about the holiday.

Extender: Leave the list on the chalkboard all day. Encourage students to add to the list during the day.

♥ How Many Holidays Can You Name?

Ask children to brainstorm holidays that occur throughout the year. Make a holiday timeline. Then have children answer the following questions using the timeline:

1. What is the first holiday in the year?
2. What is the last holiday in the year?
3. Which holiday just passed?
4. Which holiday will be celebrated next?
5. What month has the most holidays?
6. What two holidays are the closest together?

Variation: Have children work in groups and brainstorm the holidays that occur during a certain period of time. For example you could have them come up with holidays that are in October, November, and December.

❄ Signs Of Autumn

Group Activity

See how many different signs of the season your students know. Write on the chalkboard: "Things That Tell Me It Is Autumn." Organize children into groups. Provide a space on the chalkboard for each group. Ask each group to brainstorm the things that tell them that autumn is beginning. After the groups have completed their lists, have them compare the lists.

Variation: The same activity can be done for each season.

❄ Season Window Viewing

When the signs of a new season can be viewed from you window, ask chidren to line up in front of the classroom windows. As they stand there, have them brainstorm the signs that they see. Then invite children to explain what each one tells them about the season.

🎈 Birthday Scramble

At the beginning of each month, scramble the letters of the name of each child who has a birthday in that month. Have children unscramble the letters and write the names on the chalkboard.

🎈 Birthday Wishes For You

Here's a unique way for your entire class to say, "Happy Birthday" to the birthday child. Have the birthday child stand in the front of the room. Write the following sentence on the chalkboard:

On your birthday, we wish you ————————— .

Go around the room and have each student add one word to the statement:

Child 1 says: On	Child 4 says: we	Child 7 must complete
Child 2 says: your	Child 5 says: wish	the sentence
Child 3 says: birthday	Child 6 says: you	

After Child 7 completes the sentence, have Child 8 begin the sentence in the same manner.

TRIP DAYS

✣ Do You Remember This Trip?

This filler will bring back pleasant memories of school trips. Over the year, collect mementos from each trip. (These mementos can be things that the children created in reaction to the trip.) Display one memento from each trip at the front of the room. Write the name of the places visited on the chalkboard. Ask students to remember where each object came from. After each association, have children brainstorm a few memories of their trip.

✣ What Do You Think We Will See?

Write the name of a place you will visit on a piece of butcher paper. On the day before the trip, hang the paper in the classroom. Briefly describe the trip to the children. Have them brainstorm what they think they will see on the trip.

Extender: After the trip, have children compare what they thought they would see with what they actually saw.

Tickets Reproducible

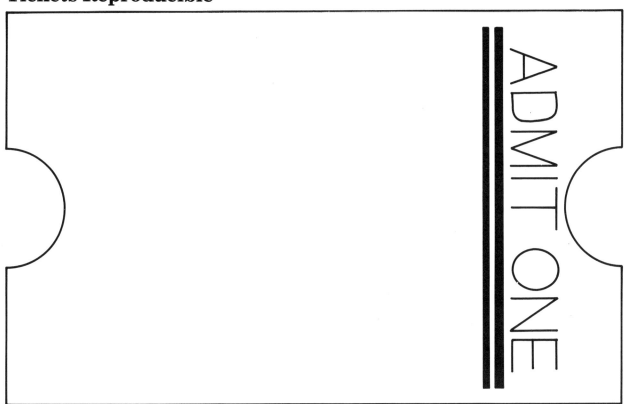

Hands Reproducible

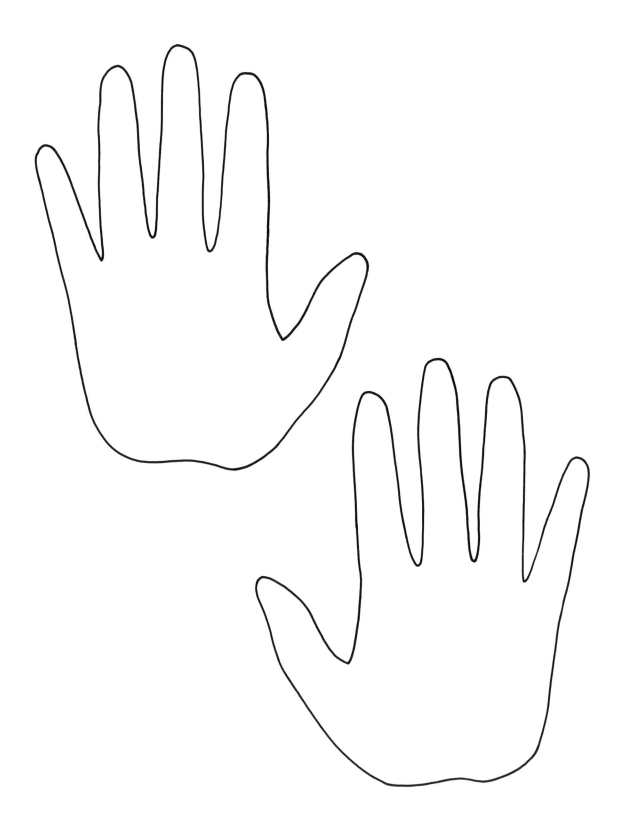

Footsteps Reproducible

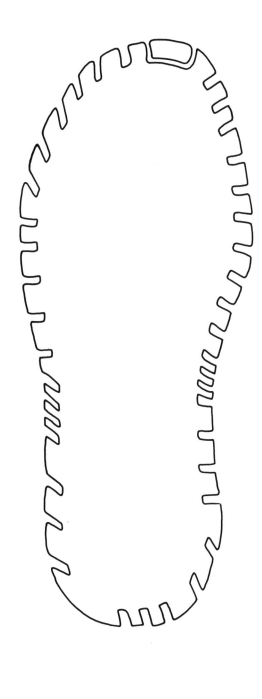

Money Reproducible

Big Tooth Reproducible

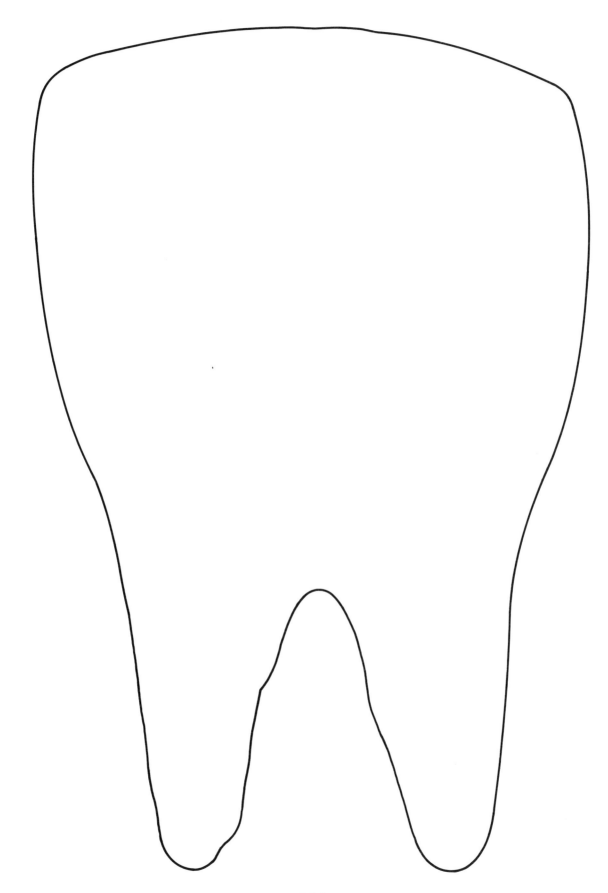

Answer Key

Welcome-Back-To-School Maze
Page 77

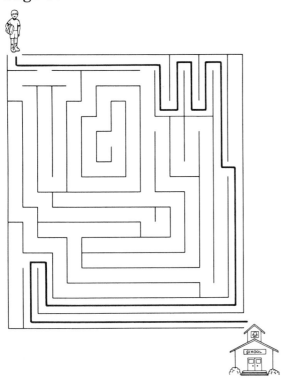

School Supply Word-Search Puzzle
Page 79

P	B	S	M	H	G	O	E	G	C	H	M	B	T	E
E	A	T	G	I	F	F	N	L	R	L	U	O	E	F
M	N	A	P	E	N	S	P	U	A	I	V	O	D	R
C	J	K	E	R	E	D	J	C	Y	B	R	K	I	U
D	A	D	N	O	T	E	B	O	O	K	S	C	C	L
M	S	C	C	Z	Y	R	W	X	N	Q	C	O	T	E
N	T	P	I	X	K	A	C	R	S	A	I	V	I	R
O	A	B	L	L	P	S	Y	Z	S	V	S	E	O	N
T	P	O	S	A	N	E	V	T	H	G	S	R	N	S
E	L	G	N	M	W	R	U	G	I	P	O	S	A	T
E	E	B	O	O	K	S	T	L	R	Q	R	A	R	A
B	R	C	I	J	K	P	Q	U	S	R	S	B	Y	P
B	D	H	E	Y	S	S	O	E	S	S	P	X	N	L
L	O	O	S	E	L	E	A	F	T	U	V	W	C	E
A	T	I	S	L	M	N	O	P	A	P	E	R	I	S

Voting-Day Maze
Page 81

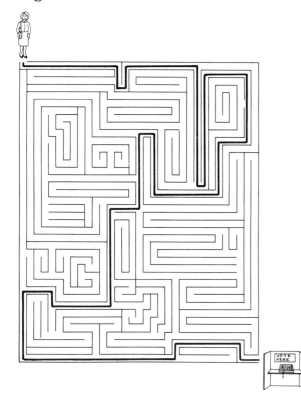

Thanksgiving Word-Search Puzzle
Page 83

I	A	D	E	P	E	T	U	R	K	E	Y	F	G	I	H	C	S
N	U	V	R	A	B	C	A	D	O	H	K	J	N	Y	A	M	T
D	E	S	P	U	M	P	K	I	N	P	I	E	X	G	Y	Z	U
I	T	F	I	T	B	K	L	N	I	J	V	W	H	E	S	D	F
A	F	U	L	U	M	N	O	D	P	L	Y	M	O	U	T	H	F
N	G	H	G	M	P	Q	X	I	W	B	X	L	A	K	A	J	I
C	I	J	R	N	V	W	H	A	R	V	E	S	T	U	C	Y	N
O	T	S	I	R	U	Y	Z	N	C	M	T	O	I	V	K	M	G
R	A	B	M	T	N	D	E	S	F	P	P	S	W	Z	S	U	T
N	M	A	S	S	A	C	H	U	S	E	T	T	S	R	E	G	Y
C	K	S	M	Y	H	N	O	G	Q	R	K	E	Y	S	T	U	P
L	R	U	N	I	T	E	D	S	T	A	T	E	S	A	U	L	I

112